Cyprus and the Financial Crisis

# Cyprus and the Financial Crisis

## The Controversial Bailout and What It Means for the Eurozone

John Theodore

and

Jonathan Theodore

First published 2015 by
PALGRAVE MACMILLAN

Palgrave Macmillan in the UK is an imprint of Macmillan Publishers Limited,
registered in England, company number 785998, of Houndmills, Basingstoke,
Hampshire RG21 6XS.

Palgrave Macmillan in the US is a division of St Martin's Press LLC,
175 Fifth Avenue, New York, NY 10010.

Palgrave Macmillan is the global academic imprint of the above companies
and has companies and representatives throughout the world.

Palgrave® and Macmillan® are registered trademarks in the United States,
the United Kingdom, Europe and other countries.

ISBN 978–1–137–45274–0

This book is printed on paper suitable for recycling and made from fully
managed and sustained forest sources. Logging, pulping and manufacturing
processes are expected to conform to the environmental regulations of the
country of origin.

A catalogue record for this book is available from the British Library.

Library of Congress Cataloging-in-Publication Data
Theodore, John, 1945–
    Cyprus and the financial crisis : the controversial bailout and what
  it means for the eurozone / John Theodore, Jonathan Theodore.
      pages   cm
    ISBN 978–1–137–45274–0 (hardback)
    1. Cyprus—Economic conditions—21st century.   2. Finance—
  Cyprus—History—21st century.   3. Banks and banking—
  Cyprus—History—21st century.   4. European Union countries—
  Foreign economic relations—Cyprus.   5. Cyprus—Foreign
  economic relations—European Union countries.   I. Theodore,
  Jonathan, 1985–   II. Title.
    HC415.2.T42 2015
    330.95693—dc23                                    2015002670

*This book is dedicated to all Cypriots and their hopes and aspirations for a better economic and united political future.*

# Contents

# Foreword

Several years after the onset of the world economic crisis, the eurozone economy continues to stagnate, with unemployment especially high in the periphery. With weak average economic growth and overall prospects uncertain, the cost of serious policy-making and crisis management failures is rising fast, both in terms of economic welfare and political polarization. The book in your hands makes an important contribution to the kind of reflection and analysis that is needed to help in charting a sustainable way forward.

This debate about the origins and the management of the eurozone crisis needs to be carried out along three different axes, which have not always received the merited equal attention. First, and most frequently discussed, is the narrative of policy-making failures at the national member-state level in terms of heavy public and private indebtedness and declining external competitiveness. Second, the shortcomings in the design of the monetary union which the crisis brought to the surface but whose share in the blame for the crisis has attracted relatively little attention; and third, the mismanagement of the crisis by the eurozone leadership that has sent the necessary correction the wrong way. The origins and management of both the Greek and Cypriot crises provide vivid illustrations in all three areas.

In the fifty years since independence in 1960, Cyprus had avoided major economic policy errors. In the context of a sound public/private sector partnership, Cyprus took advantage of external opportunities to build a strong service-oriented economy based on export. In parallel, during the process of joining institutions with sound economic practices such as the WTO, the EU and the eurozone, Cyprus implemented several much needed economic and structural reforms. But the arrival of the eurozone crisis found the country with serious pre-existing and homegrown imbalances.

The substantial increase in capital inflows, encouraged first by the prospect and then by the actual entry into the EU and the eurozone, together with the narrow emphasis of the Maastricht criteria on fiscal performance rather than on also monitoring the potentially destabilising activities of the private sector, and on nominal rather than real convergence to the better-performing member-states, set the stage for eventual trouble. National policymakers and external analysts failed to realize that dangerous imbalances could lurk beneath an apparently stable macroeconomic surface. Actual output was growing at its potential rate, inflation was low and stable and unemployment was at its natural rate, despite significant economic migration. But the structure of output was in fact unsustainable due to excessive investment in the construction sector.

At the same time excessive bank credit expansion supported by capital inflows and excessively leveraged financial institutions, led to a build-up of large household and business indebtedness, and high-risk investments. Poor bank corporate governance was largely unchecked by the Central Bank because of the widespread and ECB – supported philosophy of 'light touch' supervision. Rising money wages without productivity or quality improvements led a significant erosion of external competitiveness. When in five short years between 2007 and 2012, through unprecedented fiscal laxity, the best fiscal performer in the eurozone was transformed into one of the worst and Cypriot government debt rose sharply from 48% to 75% of GDP, Cyprus was faced with a homegrown deadly combination of banking and fiscal irresponsibility. By 2012, Cyprus was deep into the trap of mutually reinforcing sovereign and banking risks: weak public finances unable to support banks needing capital and banks underestimating risk, getting into trouble and, thereby, undermining the sustainability of public finances.

The period 2011–2012 was characterized by a number of missed opportunities to conclude agreement on an EU support program and minimize the impact of this adverse loop between the sovereign and the banks. This could have been done as early as May 2011 when Cyprus was shut out of financial markets, or in October 2011 when the Greek PSI resulted in huge losses for the two largest Cypriot banks, and finally in the second half of 2012 when endless disputes over relatively unimportant items in a draft Memorandum of Understanding delayed an agreement until it was too late to save the banks. By the time the new government took office in March 2013, the deposit outflows of the previous several months of uncertainly, and the worsening of the quality of bank portfolios, raised the capital requirements of the banks to much higher levels than was the case just a few months earlier. This led Cyprus' official creditors to the conclusion that the country could not sustain borrowing the full amount of its required rescue package.

The thrust of the rationale for the 'bail-in' of depositors was that taxpayers should not have to bear the full cost of the policy failures and bank excesses outlined above. Furthermore, the argument went, some of the depositors sharing in rescuing the Cyprus economy included Russian 'oligarchs' taking advantage of a 'tax haven' and perhaps engaging in 'money laundering'. Moreover, according to this viewpoint, the 'bail-in' would help reduce significantly the size of the unsustainably large Cypriot financial services sector and, if successfully implemented, send a message of market discipline to depositors everywhere in the eurozone.

A proposal to 'bail-in' a relatively small part of deposits in all banks from all depositors was rejected by Cypriot law makers and was followed by the imposition of a much more drastic solution involving the closing of Laiki Bank and the exchange of almost half the uninsured deposits into shares at the Bank of Cyprus. As should have been expected, confidence in the banking system was shuttered and capital controls were imposed. Although the impact on the economy was not as severe as had been feared, at present we are not in a position to know if the impact of this solution on debt sustainability is any better than if the whole amount needed was loaned to Cyprus. Future economic historians might be able to throw more light on this issue.

While several of the newer member countries missed the opportunity of eurozone membership to reform their domestic structures to achieve real convergence with the market-based economies of the North, and suffered the consequences, 'design faults' of the Monetary Union have also contributed to the troubles of the eurozone. Substantial capital flows from surplus economies have sustained large and persistent imbalances in deficit countries masking lagging competitiveness and increasing financial vulnerability. Furthermore, these capital inflows facilitated excessive domestic bank credit expansion and unsustainable real estate bubbles. These developments exposed the assumption implicit in the architecture of the monetary union that threats to stability could only come from the public sector. The lack of focus on surveillance of private bank credit expansion rates and competitiveness indicators, together with the lack of policy coordination and the possibility of exchange rate adjustments, allowed current account imbalances in several countries to reach unsustainable levels.

When it comes to correcting these large imbalances, the refusal of Germany in particular but also other surplus countries, to expand domestic demand means that the only alternative option is through 'internal devaluation' in deficit countries. Full reliance on this mechanism has proven to be not only extremely painful but also very slow. It is now increasingly recognized in Europe that the 'repair agenda' needs to be a two-way process; the fiscally stronger countries of the North, many with large current account surpluses, should make a greater contribution to economic rebalancing in the eurozone through a domestic demand boost, thereby giving a chance to economic adjustment and reforms in the indebted countries of the periphery to succeed. This is not currently in the 'rule book' of the monetary union, but it ought to be.

Another key 'design fault', which is being corrected through a painfully slow process, is the absence of a banking union, which has exposed the potentially lethal interdependence between governments and the banking system. As noted above in the case of Cyprus, potentially insolvent national banks, under inadequate national supervision, become a sovereign liability, while these banks are exposed to the risk of holding their governments' debt. The potentially disastrous impact of this interdependence is compounded by the lack of access of governments to borrowing from their national banks. This provision can easily turn a liquidity crisis into a solvency crisis when governments lose access to international financial markets to cover national liquidity shortages.

In early 2010 European leaders and the eurozone institutions were faced with a crisis of large in balances built over the years which they were not expecting and were not prepared to deal with. Because of the design gaps in the monetary union there were no agreed rules for managing a crisis. Economic decisions were taken with political criteria, sometimes connected with the electoral cycle in powerful countries. The Greek PSI and the Cyprus bail-in stand out. They respectively introduced credit risk in euro area sovereign debt and raised the cost of borrowing, and risk in the safety of bank deposits putting additional pressures in banks in the periphery. Initiatives such as the European Stability Mechanism, the ECB's Outright

Monetary Transactions and 'whatever it takes' declarations are all attempts to strengthen the crisis management capabilities of the monetary union – but they have done too little to improve the health of the European banking system, growth prospects and the state of unemployment, which remain serious challenges.

The crisis in the eurozone is a mixture of self-inflicted wounds and systemic failures.

In deficit countries structural reform needs to accelerate to help achieve greater real convergence, while in surplus countries domestic demand needs to expand contributing to the imbalance repair agenda. Beyond these short-term imperatives, the improvement in the design of the monetary union through the creation of the banking union, needs to the complemented by robust mechanisms to identify and limit macroprudential credit expansion risks, and monitor competitiveness divergences. And ultimately, when sufficient progress towards political union is achieved, put in place a fiscal governance system that complements preventive surveillance at the national level with collective fiscal support in response to shocks, as is done in truly federal systems. As already mentioned above, in the case of Cyprus the jury is still out on whether the bail-in solution was a rational attempt to re-balance the Cypriot economy or a more expensive alternative to a conventional 'bail-out'.

Building on the authors' legal and historical background and interest in history, the book presents the current financial crisis through the prism of the most significant episodes in Cyprus' modern history.

Dr Michael Sarris
Ex Minister of Finance

# Preface and Acknowledgements

This is a book about the events leading up to and the recent Cyprus eurozone financial crisis and its aftermath. Nothing from the Cypriot perspective, of any substantial size, has been written about the recent (and unexpected) financial crisis on the island, or of the unprecedented way in which the eurozone reacted, with its controversially draconian bailout terms that impacted the whole population.

Between 2011 and 2013, Cyprus experienced crippling financial problems in the fallout from the debt crisis in Greece, a country with which it had deep economic ties. In the months that followed, it implemented a host of austerity measures, including a controversial and unprecedented one-time levy on all uninsured bank deposits. The Cypriot crisis differentiates from the other PIGS bailouts in that it created a precedent contrary to international banking practices. For the very first time, depositors (local residents as well as non-Cypriot nationals) were included (contrary to EU law) in the stringent terms of the bailout provisions.

The aim of this book is to assist in providing a broader viewpoint on these ongoing issues, framing them in the context of the wider Cypriot historical experience since the invasion, using it as a lens to examine the unravelling financial relationship between Cyprus, Greece, Russia and the institutions of the eurozone. The book focuses on qualitative research through face-to-face high-level interviews with Cypriot business leaders, politicians, and academics. It incorporates the views of leading protagonists in the Cyprus government and banking sectors, as well as opinions from throughout the EU, and the considerable wealth of data concerning the policies of its many institutions and associated entities, both public and private.

\* \* \*

We would like to express our deep thanks to all those who have kindly given us their valuable time in helping us to record the events surrounding the financial crisis in Cyprus – especially for the insight into the months leading up, during, and immediately after the rescue plan.

In no particular order we extend our sincere gratitude to Michael Sarris, Christis Christoforou, Andreas Artemis, Yiannis Kypri, Christos Triantafyllides, Michalis Antoniou, Eleni Marianou, Demetris Zorbas, Chris Hadjisoteriou, Michael Papamichael, Robert Clarke and officials at the European Commission for their patience in explaining the details of the events as they saw them at the time. We would like to thank Manchester Metropolitan University for providing financial support for the project.

We would also like to offer a very special thanks to George Pantelides of Deloitte for coordinating the arrangements for many of the interviews that took place in June 2014.

Further thanks go to Barbara, the wife of John, who has provided patience and sympathy in the critical months prior to producing the manuscript, and finally to the many Cypriots who shared their views on the individual, personal, and human impacts the events of 2013 had on their families and lives.

# About the Authors

**John** Theodore is a trained barrister who has published in International law journals. He has spent over 30 years of his professional working life internationally on EU funded projects and leading teams from the UK university and banking sector advising businesses across Europe. He has been a speaker at the Committee of the Regions in Brussels and in recent years an adviser on business tourism to a number of MEPs in Brussels. He has also been an adviser and visiting professor at Warsaw University of Applied Sciences where he was awarded the Senate Medal of Merit.

**Jonathan** Theodore graduated from Christ Church Oxford with a First in Modern History together with a postgraduate Master's, where he also edited Cherwell. He has recently completed a PhD at King's College London, where he has been an undergraduate tutor in Roman and Medieval history for three years. Apart from a number of consultancy assignments for companies engaged in research for the creative industries he has also worked with a university led initiative advising a group of MEPs to support SME growth in their constituencies.

# Introduction

In May 2013, Cyprus, an Eastern Mediterranean island populated by less than a million people and the third smallest economy in the eurozone, took over the headlines around the world, focusing the minds of investors from New York to London to Hong Kong. Nearly a year after it suffered devastating losses to its banking system in a desperate political arrangement to save Greece, Brussels offered Cyprus a financial *Sophie's Choice*: either the island accepts punitive rescue terms, tantamount to a mass raid on saving accounts, or it goes under.

For several years, the economic condition of the island – long a poster child for posterity at the hand of international finance – had started to deteriorate. The decline of tourism and shipping as a result of the slowdown in Europe contributed to a contraction of the Cypriot economy in two recessions after 2008, and rising unemployment. The deficit spiralled rapidly under a new government with ambitious social programmes. Cypriot banks had amassed about 22 billion euros in Greek private sector debt. Under the terms of the Private Sector Involvement (PSI) programme rescue package for that country, they took a massive loss, and the banking sector faced almost immediate collapse. Shut out of international markets due to deteriorating state finances, and relying on a temporary Russian loan for life support, the Cypriot government requested a bailout from the EU – joining a chorus of afflicted nations that since 2010 has included Portugal, Ireland, Spain and Greece.

The deal on the table threatened to destroy the island's financial sector – the engine of its economy, alongside tourism, and the agent of a remarkable era of growth – and went so far as to violate the entire

1

principle of deposit safety that is at the heart of the fractional reserve banking system. Yet, at the same time, these measures were argued by the ruling bodies of the EU to not only be necessary, but also justified in some moral sense – punishment for the island's reckless ties to unsavoury Russian capital, and a greedy gorge on Greek debt.

The question of what happened on the island and how it was managed internationally may appear superfluous to some, given the country is relatively small and has been bailed out, but the resolution of the situation will set historical precedents that could – and, we will argue, will – take on massive importance if other peripherals, particularly Spain and Italy, face serious problems in both the banking sectors and state finances.

Cyprus has been an experiment for the eurozone. At some point between March 4 and 6, 2013, a decision was made – very likely in Berlin – to impose a depositor 'bail-in' for the first time on a eurozone crisis state. Cyprus would have to supplement its €10bn rescue loan with a widespread seizure of bank savings – a move virtually without precedent in first-world finance since the bank busts of the Great Depression. The Troika has claimed that these measures were not intended to set any precedent even though a wealth of evidence suggests precisely the opposite.

This book plots a course through the landmarks of Cyprus's recent past since independence. It charts the progress of the island from an economic backwater ravaged by war into a booming hub of international commerce, despite or even because of the political upheavals created by intercommunal and internecine warfare. The authors draw on a number of extensive discussions with relevant parties in Cyprus and around the eurozone.

This book aims to present the financial crisis first and foremost through the prism of the common (Greek) Cypriot historical experience since the 1960s. In this respect, its timeline stretches back further than most direct considerations of a financial crash. This is for a very good reason. It is a central contention of this work that the recent catastrophe for Cyprus did not emerge from a historical vacuum, but comes off the back of one of the longest ethnic conflicts in the world. The psychological trauma of the invasion played no small role in pushing Greek Cypriots into the arms of those supranational institutions and partners they believed could guarantee their security and prosperity, where the guarantors of the 1960 terms of independence had so spectacularly failed them. Economic success proved an alluring alternative to the ruined promise of political unity.

The historical irony of this path, forged with both security and prosperity in mind, is that the new financial networks Cyprus formed, internationally, through the eurozone, and especially with its blood brother Greece, would – through a particular chain of events – go on to wreck the fortunes and stability of the island nation more rapidly than anything since events of 1974. It was the financial crisis of 2013 that almost destroyed an economy that in the preceding forty years had survived invasion, partition and intercommunal civil war.

The book will attempt to strip out the most salient causal events of this process: in relation to internal Cypriot history, Mediterranean and Great Power, and the economic forces at work in the European debt crisis. It will identify the milestones that have influenced the development of the island in its quest for both political and economic solutions to the problems brought about by its flawed independence arrangements from 1960, through to its rise as an international financial centre, its accession to the EU in 2004, and the eurozone in 2008.

Tied to this are wider questions about the future of the eurozone, and the political and financial institutions that act as its guarantors. The health of the European financial system is intimately tied to the well-being of European states, as manifest in holdings of sovereign debt. Europe is now facing the longest period of sustained unemployment, slow growth and financial crunch in its modern history. Within a global economy poised between recovery and crisis, the eurozone is performing consistently worse than its neighbours and competitors, and its prospects remain uncertain.

With its strategic proximity to the Middle East, Cyprus has long been a crucible of the Mediterranean, coveted by many powers over the centuries for its unique position and nesting at the crossroads of the Europe, Asia and the Islamic world; it has been rivalled in its geopolitical importance only by Malta. The island has been a hub of international traffic for centuries – whether ships, armies, trade or, most recently, flows of tax-shy capital. It is no coincidence that with its position at the arteries of the Mediterranean, and with no abundance of natural resources save for idyllic weather and beautiful beaches, Cyprus would wish to capitalise on its unique geostrategic position to investors to sell its expertise in terms of legal and financial services, based on the post-imperial traditions of English common law that were a baseline standard throughout the commercial world. That the island nation was ripped in two in 1974 added urgency to these endeavours. Dealing with the consequences of invasion became its greatest challenge until 2013.

Although tourism and then shipping became an important part of the Republic's drivers for economic growth, these were dwarfed in the 1990s and beyond when its economy was transformed into a major offshore financial centre. Cyprus has been a tax haven since the 1970s. At first, it kept taxes low to attract shipping companies that registered their ships in Limassol. The focus of this 'financialisation' was encouraged in part by the desire to develop its banking and financial ties with Greece to which it had a deeply ingrained cultural history, a common psychological bond, and mutual security needs with respect to Turkey. But the big boom in this process came after the collapse of the Soviet Union, and the creation of a new class of wealthy elite from its ashes. The billions made out of the dubious privatisations of that era needed a safe haven – for political as much as financial reasons - and found it in the small nation.

Cyprus enjoyed around 35 years of almost continuous and robust growth with a booming housing market, foreign investment and tourism. From 2010, however, the nation's debt problems grew fast. Its banking sector rapidly crumbled after the Greek PSI deal of October 2011 and April 2012, which wiped out most of their extensive bond holdings. The government also failed to take action soon enough when the crisis was escalating, as will be discussed in Chapters Two and Three: they could and should have negotiated assistance in the summer of 2011 or 2012, instead of completing the negotiations in March 2013.

There is a particular narrative about the crisis that has been sold by Brussels to the wider public of the EU. It is one that makes Cyprus sound exceptional and unique – a tiny island which attracted illicit wealth, was overrun with the corrupt spoils of Russian oligarchs, and got burned by its own greed. It was an easy and attractive story to sell to the European media. Many, in fact, bought it. And it would be wrong to say that there is absolutely no truth in it at all.

However, it is also a story that is remarkably limited and misleading. It is one which ignores so many facts that contributed, in greater or lesser measure, to the crisis: the role of the regulatory infrastructure of the eurozone, the Cyprus-unfriendly peculiarities of the Greek PSI, the role of the communist government on the island, a devastating industrial accident, and the psychological and economic principles of Enosis that help explain the massive concentration of Greek debt in Cypriot hands. All these are dealt with at length in this book.

The Cypriot debt crisis has seen a controversial new form 'bail-in' package, provoked popular outbursts in the streets, and required tense political negotiating in the eurozone. However, it is only one part of a larger problem of economic stability and political unity facing the European Union today. The relationship of those issues to the island's recent history is central to the purpose of this book. In particular, it seeks to make clear just how useful and convenient Cyprus was to test a new bailout strategy in the eurozone – an economic entity still defined by suffocating debt levels, which the threat of oncoming deflation will only exacerbate.

# 1
## Birth of a Nation

### The Road to Independence

In this chapter we need to examine some of the key landmarks that have helped to influence events in the island's most recent history and its attempts at authentic self-determination: sovereignty backed by protectorates, but thwarted by the complexities of the constitutional arrangement, the ethnic and cultural makeup of the island, and wider geopolitical pressures. It is important here to unravel how Greek Cyprus – both its elites and ordinary citizens – reacted to the breakdown of the system of power-sharing after 1963, and to the constant threats to its security that followed: most important, the 1974 invasions and its consequences. The reaction to these threats took different forms. Key to this response in political terms was the successful internationalisation of the island's problems through the United Nations in New York. This was led by then president, Archbishop Makarios, who displayed an acute ability at playing off domestically one party against another to maintain his position as the elected head of government. Beyond that, it was to show the world that it could mirror the success of other island states in the provision of financial services to the international community: exploiting its constitutional foundation in British common law and appealing particularly to those geographically proximate clients from Russian and Eastern Europe, where banking laws were not as developed as in the west.

Many Cypriots sought the incorporation of Cyprus into Greece when Greece became independent in 1830, but the island itself remained part of the Ottoman Empire. The Russo-Turkish war of 1878 ended its direct rule over Cyprus; the sovereignty of the island continued to belong to Ottoman Empire until Britain annexed the island unilaterally in 1914, when it declared war against the Ottomans at the First World War. Following World War I, under the provisions of the Lausanne Treaty, Turkey relinquished all claims and rights on Cyprus. With the dissolution of the Ottoman Empire, the island was made a Crown Colony in 1925.

The period immediately before independence in 1960 was marked on the Greek Cypriot side by a 'war' of liberation against British colonial rule – mirroring those that took place in other countries seeking independence, but with additional dimensions related to the ethnic history of the island, and its strategic location in the Eastern Mediterranean. The war of liberation and the imposition on Cyprus of one of the world's most complex constitutions set the scene for a turbulent and tragic phase of history, from which the island has only partly recovered. The difficulties the fledgling new state faced were enormous, and the vested strategic interests of Greece, Turkey, Britain and – most importantly – the United States were to fatally compromise its survival in a complete, intact form.

On the island itself, there was not only inter-communal wrangling between Greek and Turkish Cypriots, but also clear divisions among the Greek Cypriots themselves on the form that political self-determination would take: whether it be as an independent republic, or linked by *enosis* (union) with Greece. The role of these different factions vying for their national interests did very little to forge a sense of security for the citizens of Cyprus, nor did it give a sense of identity and common purpose. The drive for *enosis* plays a large, though not exclusive, role in provoking the Turkish invasion – splintering even further the Greek world it had sought to bind together as one indivisible whole.

The events that followed have been well documented in numerous studies by an array of historians, lawyers, scholars and security experts. Included in this are one of the authors of this book's research and interviews over the years with leading politicians in the early years of the inter-communal conflict and senior UN officials.[1] However, the events of the last few years allow for their significance to be considered in light of events a generation later.

The psychological trauma of the invasion played no small part in pushing Greek Cypriots into the arms of those international institutions, political and financial, that could provide a better source of security and prosperity than the failed guarantees of the 1960 treaty. In the first decade of the 21$^{st}$ century, one form of union – that with the Turkish north, as put forward in the Annan Plan – was rejected, and another – membership of the European Union (EU) and later the eurozone – was avidly embraced.

In a way, the accession of Cyprus to the EU effectively meant a political and economic *enosis* with Greece within the EU apparatus. This is precisely why – to the alarm of many Turkish Cypriots – the Greek president, Costas Simitis, declared in April 2003, when Cyprus signed its Accession Treaty with the EU, that *enosis* had finally been achieved.

The historical irony of this alternative path, forged with prosperity and security in mind, is that the legal and financial infrastructure that bonded Greece and Greek Cypriot Cyprus more closely than ever before, would wreck the fortunes, finances and stability of the island nation more rapidly than anything since the invasion itself.

## Nationhood, Its Costs and Consequences

The road to independence for the island had its immediate origins in the EOKA campaign of 1955–59 to end British colonial rule.[2] EOKA, a Cypriot paramilitary organisation, fought for the island's independence 'from the British yoke' and eventual *enosis* with Greece.[3] Such was the aim of most Greek Cypriot movements, including the Communist Party of Cyprus – the forerunner of the modern AKEL party – since 1926. Britain had originally promised Cyprus to Greece in 1915 in exchange for their entry into World War I on the sides of the Allies. Although Greece did join the Allies, their entry was not immediate and the offer by Britain was not upheld. All attempts at getting support for union with Greece were then vigorously opposed by the British until the Second World War when in 1941, they offered Cyprus to Greece in return for invading Bulgaria, which had entered the war on the side of the Germans. It is noteworthy that many thousands of Cypriots volunteered to fight in the British forces as a result of these promises.

Although Greece by now had declared its support both for independence and *enosis*, events in the Eastern Mediterranean transpired to make its progress more haphazard. British foreign policy from the mid-1950s was absorbed with its Suez strategy in Egypt – and from 1956, the legacy of their disastrous intervention to occupy the Canal with France. The consequence of its failing to maintain a presence there made the government desperate to retain a strategic presence in Cyprus – if not full colonial sovereignty – as a base to pursue and maintain its foreign policy objectives in the Middle East and, especially, to help maintain an uninterrupted supply of oil from Iran and Iraq.

The retention of its military bases therefore played a dominant role in Britain's negotiations over the independence of the island. In an era that saw a rapid decline in its status as a world power, Cyprus became for Britain the last bolthole close to its political and commercial interests further east. This principle dominated their position in the pre-independence negotiations and found its stamp firmly fixed in the Treaty of Establishment of 1960.[4]

Coupled with this, both Greece and Turkey were now part of NATO, and seen as pivotal to the strategic defence of the region against the Soviet Union; consequently, their respective interests could not be ignored in the decision-making process for Cypriot self-determination.

The armed campaign, which EOKA began with a series of bombings in April 1955, continued for four years until the political wing of the organisation, led by Archbishop Makarios, agreed to abandon the ambitions of *enosis* in favour of just independence as a solution to the conflict. In February 1959 a compromise agreement along these lines was concluded between Turkish and Greek representatives at Zürich and endorsed by the Cypriot communities in London and in March 1959.[5]

On August 16, 1960 the island of Cyprus was proclaimed independent by its last British governor, Sir Hugh Foot. The new state, populated by Greek Cypriots numbering 82% of the population and Turkish Cypriots 18% had Archbishop Makarios III of Greece as its president, and Fazil Kutchuk of Turkey as its vice-president. Under the new Treaty of Establishment, derived from the Zurich and London agreements, the Sovereign Base Areas of Akrotiri and Dhekelia remained (to this day) as British Overseas Territories, covering an area of 99 square miles. Support for this arrangement was underwritten by a Treaty of Guarantee signed by Britain, Greece and Turkey, as well as a Treaty of Alliance signed by Cyprus, Greece and

Turkey. The latter unravelled soon after, when in 1963 the Turkish air force conducted a bombing raid in the area around Tylliria, following which the Republic of Cyprus announced that the Treaty was rendered null and void. As to whether these other treaties per se remain valid in international law, remains a matter of legal conjecture, deserving of more specialist attention than in this book.[6]

It is not unreasonable to point out that the agreements which confirmed the independence of Cyprus sidestepped the principle tenets of self-determination enshrined in the UN Charter by the way in which the whole negotiations for independence were conducted.[7] To what extent were the people of Cyprus involved in the process and in particular on the transfer of its sovereign territory to the colonial power? Makarios had not been at the Zurich negotiations, and in London his signature had been requested. It was suggested that there was a possibility of duress/pressure from Athens to do so but contrary views believe this not to be the case, whatever misgivings were felt at the time.[8]

Makarios, as the representative of the Greek Cypriots, offered mixed messages on the final terms of the agreement. His statement, made after the London Conference held at Lancaster House in 1959, offered a relatively upbeat view of the future of the two communities of the island:

> Yesterday I had certain reservations. In overcoming them I have done so in a spirit of trust and good-hearted good will towards the Turkish community and its leaders. It is my firm belief that with sincere understanding and mutual confidence we can work together in a way that will leave no room for dissension about any written provisions and guarantees. It is the spirit in the hearts of men that counts most. I am sure that all past differences will be completely forgotten.[9]

However the above statement seemed to differ in a later comment by Makarios that offered up more serious misgivings, when in an article on the proposed Amendments to the Cyprus constitution he remarked:

> At the Conference at Lancaster House in February 1959, which I was invited to attend as leader of Greek Cypriots, I raised a

number of objections and expressed strong misgivings regarding certain provisions of the Agreement arrived at in Zurich between the Greek and the Turkish Governments and adopted by the British Government. I tried very hard to bring about the change of at least some provisions of that Agreement. I failed, however, in that effort and I was faced with the dilemma either of signing the Agreement as it stood or of rejecting it with all the grave consequences which would have ensued. In the circumstances I had no alternative but to sign the Agreement. This was the course dictated to me by necessity.[10]

As was to be seen later in the official attempts to arrive at a permanent peaceful settlement, all parties seemed to respect the significance of Article 185 of the Constitution, stipulating that the 'territory of the Republic is one and indivisible and the complete or partial union of Cyprus with any other state is expressly excluded.'

It is not an understatement to argue that the agreement sowed the seeds for future conflict between the Greek and Turkish Cypriots. The Treaties making up the Cyprus Constitution created a unique problem on the whole issue of power-sharing by communities of unequal sizes: with the Greek Cypriots at 82% of the population and Turkish Cypriots 18%. The treaties created a complex web of checks and balances aimed at securing the protection of the minority Turkish Cypriot community (although it is worth mentioning the Armenian community and other smaller minorities were not accorded any special minority rights under the 1960 constitution). Nevertheless, its complex and unwieldy formulation may have created more problems with the effective government of the island than it resolved. Well-intentioned in principle, its bewildering array of checks and balances were almost impossible to apply in practice. Five years later, the UN Secretary General's Mediator on Cyprus, Dr Galo Plaza, described the 1960 Constitution created by the Zürich and London Agreements as 'a constitutional oddity', and noted that difficulties in implementing the treaties signed on the basis of those Agreements had begun almost immediately after independence.[11]

As constitutional expert, Professor S.A. De Smith, observed in 1964:

The Constitution of Cyprus is probably the most rigid in the world. It is certainly the most detailed and (with the possible exception of Kenya's new Constitution) the most complicated. It is weighed down by checks and balances, procedural and substantive safeguards, guarantees and prohibitions. Constitutionalism has run riot in harness with Communalism. The Government of the Republic must be carried on, but never have the chosen representatives of a political majority been set so daunting an obstacle course by the constitution makers.[12]

He further remarked that

Unique in its tortuous complexity and in the multiplicity of the safeguards that it provides for the principal majority, the Constitution of Cyprus stands alone among the constitutions of the world. Two nations dwell together under its shadow in uneasy juxtaposition, unsure whether this precariously poised structure is about to fall crashing about their ears.[13]

On the latter point, he was not proven very wrong.

## A Unified Country Breaks Down, 1963–1964

It was only a matter of time before day-to-day governmental administration became unworkable. The constitutional arrangements broke down in November 1963, when President Makarios put forward '13 points' for amending the constitution – some of which he had early raised, but been ignored on, at the London conference – to make it more workable. Fundamental to these proposals was the removal of the power of veto for both the (Greek Cypriot) president and (Turkish Cypriot) vice-president. It was the operation of the power of veto in foreign affairs, defence and internal security that seriously impeded the machinery of government in the first years of the state of Cyprus. Furthermore, Makarios called for a revision of the fixed 70:30 ratio of civil servants to something more accurately reflecting the island's demographics, and the abolition of a separate Greek and Turkish judicial system. These measures were rejected by the Turkish Cypriot vice-president and in the strongest terms by Turkey itself, which threatened intervention if the revisions were unilaterally implemented.

There was little hope of a modus vivendi between the two communities of the island. Under the constitution, both communities were given the right of maintaining special relationships with their respective 'motherlands' of Greece and Turkey. By perpetuating educational and cultural collaboration from Greece and Turkey, combined with access to financial subsidies, there was little chance of developing a common and coherent 'Cypriot' identity. This division was further entrenched when eruptions of inter-communal violence in the winter of 1963–4 led to the setting up of enclaves' where Turkish Cypriots moved out of mixed villages – many of which had seen peaceful coexistence for generations – into ethnically homogenous areas in an attempt to bolster their security. After the outbreak of violence in 1963, Turkish Cypriot politicians and public servants refused to exercise the functions of their respective offices and effectively withdrew from the Constitution, with Vice-President Küçük and ministers and members of the House of Representatives ceasing to participate in the government.[14]

This posed the problem of maintaining a functioning government in any real sense across the island. From July 1963 the Supreme Constitutional Court could not sit because its Turkish Cypriot president had resigned. A similar fate befell the High Court, which was condemned to inactivity from May 1964 following the resignation of its president. Until June 1964 the Turkish district judges also refused to attend to their duties, thereafter resuming them on a restricted basis. In the face of these pressures it was necessary to enact the Administration of Justice (Miscellaneous Provisions) Law of 1964 simply to keep the wheels of law and order in motion. The new Act made legislative provisions in respect of the exercise of the judicial power formerly exercised by the Supreme Constitutional Court and the High Court. To this end, a new Supreme Court was created consisting of between five and seven members, including all existing members of the Supreme Constitutional Court and the High Court under the chairmanship of their senior member, who happened to be Turkish Cypriot. In any event, the House of Representatives and Council of Ministers continued to operate in the absence of the Turkish Cypriot members so long as the requisite quorum for legislative and executive authority existed. Decisions continued to be taken in accordance with the provisions of the constitution until 1974.

Inter-communal fighting started in December 1963 following the breakdown of the Constitution. Fierce fighting looked as if it would result in the Turkish Cypriot quarter of Nicosia being taken over by the Greek Cypriots at which point Turkey's threat to invade Cyprus forced President Makarios to accept a ceasefire on December 25. It was agreed that this would be monitored by British troops.[15]

Turkish attempts from the mainland to invade the north of the island were thwarted not least by the determined efforts of the Lyndon Johnson administration in the United States.[16] But more importantly was the stern warning given by the Soviet leader, Khrushchev, when he said that 'The Soviet Government hereby states that if there is an armed foreign invasion of Cyprus territory, the Soviet Union will help the Republic of Cyprus to defend its freedom and independence against foreign intervention.'[17] Turkish forces, spearheaded/led by submarine activity in the Mediterranean off the Turkish coast, were halted in their tracks. Rapid and earnest UN mediation helped to establish a ceasefire, with the Security Council establishing the United Nations Peacekeeping Force in Cyprus (UNFICYP) to help prevent hostilities between Greek and Turkish Cypriot communities: an entity which is still in place today. It is a tribute to the diplomatic efforts of Archbishop Makarios – at least at this stage – to get the UN General Assembly adopting a Resolution in 1965 recognising that the Republic of Cyprus should enjoy full sovereignty and complete independence without any foreign intervention or interference.[18]

The UN's involvement was not just limited to providing boots on the ground to keep the peace.[19] It was combined with intensive mediation efforts by the duly appointed UN Mediator, Dr Galo Plaza, to forge an agreement by both sides to obtain concessions for a political solution.

The report of the UN Mediator, known as the Plaza Report, was submitted March 25, 1965. Dr Plazo argued against the partition of the island, on the grounds that it would not be economically viable and it would never be accepted by a clear majority of the population. Instead he advocated a settlement giving the Turkish Cypriots a degree of political autonomy, but not at the level accorded in the 1960 treaties. Plazo concluded that the Cyprus problem could not be solved by the restoration of the status quo ante, but through a new solution that maintained a unitary state but provided adequate safeguards, entrenched in law, for the Turkish Cypriot minority. This proposal was rejected by the Turkish Cypriot leadership, which continued to advocate a solution based on a bi-regional federation with a geographical partition. The report was also roundly rejected by the Turkish government.

Key observations about the report were offered up in in-depth interviews with the protagonists on both sides. Some representative quotes are offered below:

> The additional guarantees, they maintained, could best be obtained by providing a geographical basis for the state of affairs created by the Zurich and London Agreements. In short, they wished to be physically separated from the Greek Cypriot community. Their first inclination had been to seek this separation through the outright physical partitioning of Cyprus between the Turkish and Greek nations, of which in their opinion the Turkish and Greek Cypriot communities constituted an extension. However, 'considering that this would not be willingly agreed to by Greek and Cypriot Greeks', they modified this concept to that of creating a federal state over the physical separation of the two communities.[20]

> Their proposal envisaged a compulsory exchange of population in order to bring about a state of affairs in which each community would occupy a separate part of the island. The dividing line was in fact suggested: to run from the village of Yalia on the north-western coast through the towns of Nicosia in the centre, and Famagusta in the east. The zone lying north of this line was claimed by the Turkish Cypriot community; it is said to have an area of about 1,084 square miles or 38 per cent of the total area of the Republic ... [21]

An exchange of about 10,000 Greek families for about the same number of Turkish families was also contemplated:

> It would seem to require a compulsory movement of the people concerned – many thousands on both sides – contrary to all the enlightened principles of the present time, including those set forth in the Universal Declaration of Human Rights. Moreover,

this would be a compulsory movement of a kind that would seem likely to impose severe hardships on the families involved as it would be impossible for all of them, or perhaps even the majority of them, to obtain an exchange of land or occupation suited to their needs or experience; it would entail also an economic and social disruption which would be such as to render neither part of the country viable. Such a state of affairs would constitute a lasting, if not permanent, cause of discontent and unrest . . . [22]

The report was well received internationally. Furthermore, the Government of Cyprus immediately announced its basic agreement with the considerations and guidelines listed in the report, and declared that it was ready to accept them 'as useful and valuable contributions to the search for a final Cyprus settlement'.[23] More broadly speaking, the internationalisation of the Cyprus conflict helped to lessen the sense of insecurity and isolation among the Greek Cypriot community by highlighting to the world (both through media coverage of the near-hostilities, and institutionally via the organs of the UN) its difficulties in solving deep-rooted ethnic and cultural conflicts: problems that owed in no small measure to the role of external powers pressing their own political and strategic agendas on the island's troubled and conflicted communities.

Nevertheless, the events of 1964, with the intervention both of America and the United Nations to try and maintain a peaceful and unified island nation, produced a false feeling of confidence that a future Turkish invasion would be blocked by such powerful international allies. It was not unreasonable to that the other two 'guaranteeing powers' – Greece and the United Kingdom – would oppose unilateral military intervention. As late as the early 1970s there was an optimistic belief amongst even prominent members of the Cypriot establishment – though not necessarily universally held[24] – that Turkey would be prevented from invading the island, that Cyprus had too many powerful allies, and that the United States would never allow it. Yet the inter-communal strife remained unresolved and, with it, the underlying conditions for eventual armed intervention by Turkey. Ten years later, the foreign policy concerns of the US under Nixon and Kissinger were quite different, and the invasion was not directly opposed.[25] Diplomatic overtures failed to halt or persuade the Turkish government to cancel its carefully prepared plans for military intervention.[26]

Following the Turkish threat to intervene, in June of 1964 Washington launched an independent initiative under former Secretary of State Dean Acheson. In July he presented a plan to unite Cyprus with Greece. In return for accepting this, Turkey would receive a sovereign military base on the island; the Turkish Cypriots would also be given minority rights, which would be overseen by a resident international commissioner. Unfortunately this proposal was rejected by Makarios, as he believed that leaving Turkey with this strategic position would give them too much power in the island's affairs, thereby limiting full *enosis*. A second version of the plan was presented that offered Turkey a 50-year lease on a base which was again unacceptable.[27]

In May 1968, after several abortive efforts in the preceding years, renewed talks began in earnest between the two sides under the auspices of the good offices of the UN Secretary-General. Unusually, the talks were not held between President Makarios and Vice-President Küçük. Instead they were conducted by the presidents of the communal chambers, Glafcos Clerides and Rauf Denktaş: both well known to each other socially and as lawyers working in Nicosia. During the first round of discussions until August, the Turkish Cypriots were prepared to make several concessions regarding constitutional matters, but Makarios refused to grant them greater autonomy in return. The second round of talks, which focused on local government, was equally unsuccessful. In December 1969 a third round of discussion started. This time they focused on constitutional issues. Yet again there was little progress and when they ended in September 1970 the Secretary-General blamed both sides for the lack of movement.

In July 1972, the author was granted interviews with Glafcos Clerides and Rauf Denktash: respectively representing the Greek Cypriot and Turkish Cypriot sides in talks to negotiate a final one-state solution to the regional hostilities that had, by this point, plagued the island state since its inception twelve years earlier. The negotiations centred on relative levels of local government control by each community and their proportional representation in the legal and political systems of the nation. From these meetings it was clear that progress was being made and could be built on as part of an overall conflict resolution. Clerides, as chief interlocutor

for the Greek Cypriot side (and president of the House of Representatives), had made progress on discussions on a number of issues,
including the formula and mechanism by which power would be
devolved to local Greek and Turkish communities. Both Greek and
Turkish Cypriots would be allowed to remain in their separate villages and townships with an autonomous local government – but
as part of a whole, non-partitioned state. The administrative scope of
this devolution would actually have been more limited than that proposed in the terms of the Annan plan 30 years later. Unfortunately,
broad-ranging concessions of power were not accepted by President
Makarios, who understandably rejected any arrangements perceived
as a quasi-federal solution, but which did not seem to accommodate the bi-communal nature of the state championed by the Turkish
Cypriot side.[28] The conflicted agendas of Greece, Turkey and the
United Kingdom overshadowed the talks, hampering and vetoing
the negotiation process even further. Local government autonomy
was non-negotiable for the Turkish side. It allowed them a sense of
ownership to affect their claim as 'co-founders' of the Republic and
co-signatories of the 1960 Constitution, instead of merely having the
status of a protected minority.[29] This issue created an insurmountable
impasse between the two sides, and these talks ground to a halt by
1974.

# 2
# Forever Divided?

## The Turkish Invasion and Its Aftermath

From 1960, monumental hurdles had confronted both the Cypriot leadership and the social and ethnical communities of the newly independent island. These festering and unresolved tensions came to a head in July 1974, when Turkey invoked its rights under the Treaty of Guarantee to take military action and invade the island on behalf of the Turkish community. A possibility that had overshadowed Cypriot affairs and the inter-communal talks since the island's independence, it was finally prompted by a coup d'etat against the government of Archbishop Makarios by the Greek military Junta: staged by the Cypriot National Guard and in conjunction with EOKA. The coup successfully deposed the Cypriot President Makarios and installed as his replacement Nikos Sampson, a leader strongly in favour of *enosis* with Greece.[1,2]

The avowedly nationalistic Junta had come to power in Greece in a military coup of their own in 1967. Their official justification was that a 'communist conspiracy' had infiltrated Greece's government, press and military, meaning that drastic action was needed to protect the country from a 'Red' takeover. The actions of the Junta were widely condemned throughout Europe, but more mildly so in the United Kingdom, which spoke out on the issue of human rights but otherwise emphasised the country's strategic value for NATO in the Mediterranean.[3] The Junta received considerable support from the United States, both publically and in more covert form.[4] This was entirely in line with Cold War strategic policy: since 1947, when the

US formulated the Truman Doctrine, the country has actively sup-
ported authoritarian governments in Greece, Turkey, Iran and the
Far East (including South Vietnam) to ensure they did not fall under
Soviet influence.

The Junta paid close attention to affairs on Cyprus, with an eye to
speedy political and territorial union of the two countries. It appears
that its ruling elements believed Makarios to have communist sym-
pathies, leading them to covertly support EOKA and dissidents in
the National Guard as they tried to undermine Makarios.[5] On July 2,
1974, the Cypriot president wrote an open letter to President Gizikis
complaining bluntly that 'cadres of the Greek military regime support
and direct the activities of EOKA.' He also ordered that Greece remove
some 600 Greek officers in the Cypriot National Guard from Cyprus.[6]
The Greek Government's immediate reply was to order the go-ahead
of the coup. On July 15, 1974 sections of the Cypriot National Guard,
led by its Greek officers, overthrew the government.[7]

Turkey immediately applied to Britain as a signatory of the Treaty
of Guarantee to take action to return Cyprus to its neutral status.
Britain declined this offer, and refused to let Turkey use its bases
on Cyprus as part of the operation. Beyond this, however, its direct
support for the island was essentially non-existent. In July 1974,
Turkish forces invaded and captured a narrow strip of the coastline
between Kyrenia and Nicosia before an initial, UN-supervised, ceasefire was declared. The operation, codenamed 'Operation Atilla', is
known in the North as 'the 1974 Peace Operation'. Ankara claimed
that it was invoking its right under the Treaty of Guarantee to protect
the Turkish Cypriots and guarantee the independence of Cyprus.[8]
The Greek military Junta rapidly collapsed and was replaced by a
democratic government. In August 1974, a second Turkish invasion
resulted in the capture of 40% of the island. The ceasefire line from
August 1974 became the United States Buffer Zone in Cyprus: referred
to as the Green Line, or more colloquially the 'Attila Line', which
stretched 180 kilometres from east to west across the island and
still divides the island. The UN Mandate meant the maintenance of
the status quo by controlling this border.[9] This line was exclusively
patrolled by the UNFICYP according to the terms of the ceasefire
arrangements called for by the Security Council Resolutions 353, 354,
355 and 360 (1974).[10]

In 1983 the Turkish Cypriot Assembly declared unilateral independence of the occupied zone as the Turkish Republic of Northern

Cyprus (TRNC). The UN Security Council, in a meeting convened by the UK, immediately declared this new entity 'legally invalid', and to this day no government or international institution other than Turkey has recognised it.

More than one quarter of the population of Cyprus was rapidly expelled from the occupied northern part of the island, where Greek Cypriots had totalled 80% of the population. There was conversely a flow of 60,000 Turkish Cypriots from the south to the north in the year after the conflict. To this day, the international community considers the territory north of the UN line to be that of the Republic of Cyprus, illegally occupied by the Turkish forces.

On the 1st of November 1974, the UN Security Council called for the immediate and unconditional withdrawal of all foreign troops from Cypriot soil, and the return of displaced refugees to their homes. This resolution has never been implemented (as with countless others including Resolution 186) by Turkey or the Turkish Cypriot Republic, on the grounds that such a measured withdrawal would have resulted in the inter-ethnic violence and persecution they claim the invasion averted. Consequently, around 40,000 Turkish troops remain in the north of the island.

In military terms the Greek Cypriot side was heavily outgunned. The invading forces numbered over 40,000 troops, 300 tanks and featured total air superiority. 'Events on the ground were very confusing', remarked Chris Hadjisoteriou when serving in a commando unit near Myrtou, 'there was a lot of military confusion on both sides and local commanders were unable to make decisions. Tragic mistakes were made when Greek forces were shot down by friendly fire.' Similar mistakes were made by the other side.[11]

The campaigns of July and August 1974 saw the Greek Cypriots isolated from international aid or support. Their purported champion, Greece, could logistically only provide limited military assistance, owing to the significant distance geographically between the two countries. Greece in 1967 had been forced to withdraw its division of 10,000 troops plus heavy weapons so there was no parity of forces in the conflict. The Turks were opposed by lightly armed forces – with a few obsolete Russian T34 tanks – on the Greek Cypriot side supported by the Greek brigade, the military presence permitted under the 1960 Constitution. In addition, Greece had its own political problems resulting from the overthrow of the Junta. Nevertheless, the limited Greek forces on the island that were maintained there under the terms of the Treaty of Guarantee helped to bolster resistance to the invasion, particularly around the perimeter of the Nicosia international airport.[12]

It is not the purpose of this book to re-examine the legality of the invasion, or the plentiful literature already available on the subject. Nor is it our intention to interpret whether the perceived rights of unilateral intervention under the treaty were a breach of the treaty – and international law – as a large section of the international legal community believed to be the case.[13] Where the legality of the invasion *can* be challenged is in whether its outcome safeguarded – as Turkey stated as its intention – the bi-communal 'consociationalism'(or power sharing), independence, sovereignty and territorial integrity of the Republic of Cyprus. Evidently, it did not: and it resulted in the de facto partition that remains in place today. Furthermore, the three guaranteeing powers (Greece, Turkey and the UK) were under an obligation to prevent 'either the union of the Republic of Cyprus with any other State, or the *partition of the Island*' (emphasis added). A justification for intervention can at least be attempted on the former point, with the *Junta* coup – but not the latter one. The grounds for armed intervention were tightly fixed by these parameters – 'In so far as common or concerted action may prove impossible, each of the three guaranteeing Powers reserves the right to take action with the sole aim of *re-establishing the state of affairs established in the present Treaty*.' (Emphasis added.)

What is important here is to trace with hindsight how in practice Cypriots dealt with their fears and insecurities created by the new de facto situation. The main thrust of the Treaty of Guarantee was for *concerted*, not unilateral, action by the guarantors – and only to restore the status quo ante. With hindsight we know this was not going to happen, and events proved this to be the case.[14]

Under the arrangements of the 1960 constitution, Greece, Turkey and the United Kingdom were guaranteeing powers of the sovereign inviolability of Cyprus. The events of the summer of 1974 made this arrangement effectively obsolete, for a number of reasons. Firstly, there was the Junta's complicity in conspiring with the forces opposed to President Makarios. This gave the pretext and the questionable legal premise for the invasion. With a government that rapidly disintegrated following the invasion and limited mobilised military resources, and now busily engaged in restoring democracy in Athens, Greece could offer little rapid or direct aid at the time. Nor could any help be forthcoming from NATO. The principle of collective defence, enshrined in Article V of the treaty was not relevant: Cyprus was not a member of NATO even though the guarantor powers of the island's security *were*.[15] Indeed, collective efforts by NATO to solve the crisis, whether through diplomacy or other sanction, had been singularly lacking.

Britain's military capability as a realistic buffer to the Turkish invasion was not inconsiderable: it had 9000 troops in the Sovereign Base Areas of the island (at Akrotiri, the airbase and the army base at Akrotiri) and air power capability to intercept Turkish jets.[16] But the Labour government that took office in March 1974 came in with a clear agenda to slash defence spending and was in no mood to flex its muscles militarily. They did send a small naval task force, led by assault carrier Hermes, to Cyprus on July 16, 1974 – the day after the coup against Makarios had begun and just four days before the Turkish invasion. But there was little appetite for unilateral action by Britain to prevent the invasion once it was underway. An offer of US support, however, would have changed everything. Decades later, Lord Callaghan privately admitted that Britain sent a task force to Cyprus in the hope of taking joint military action with the United States to deter a Turkish invasion. 'It was the most frightening moment of my career,' he said. 'We nearly went to war with Turkey. But the Americans stopped us.'[17]

In purely practical terms, sole direct intervention by the United Kingdom may have achieved little: in the event that there had been engagement with the invading forces the British garrisons would have been outnumbered about 4:1 in manpower alone, not to mention the dominance of Turkish heavy armour.[18] Harold Wilson's Labour administration was only prepared to act with the Americans, with James Callaghan stating that 'if the American Sixth Fleet and elements of the British Navy had put themselves between the Turkish mainland and Cyprus, the Turks could have decided to back off.' Post Suez, the British Government showed an extreme reluctance to take any military stance in the region (without the blessing of the United States) to invoke prior treaty obligations. There was already concern that Greece and Turkey, both members of NATO, were mobilising for a direct or proxy conflict (Greece had called for a total mobilisation in response to the invasion) and with Britain, a further NATO member taking a more direct part events could have escalated into an all-out Mediterranean war. For Britain, there was no enthusiasm to engage with the Turks unless in concert with the Americans. Both they and the US could claim that the anti-Makarios coup was the *casus belli* of the invasion, and not their own inability or unwillingness to halt it in the first place.

Such reasoning would not spare the government intense political criticism at home. MPs in Parliament repeatedly challenged the foreign secretary James Callaghan on why Britain, as a guarantor of Cyprus's independence, failed to take action to mitigate the crisis or substantially aid in the Greek Cypriot defence: with its military bases at Akrotiri and Dekelia, strategic listening posts on Troodos Mount Olympus, and substantial garrison presence. Only with forensic examination of the political and diplomatic documents would true light be thrown on the real intentions of the parties at the time. As one politician said at the time, 'The full truth will never be known unless, and until, all official papers of the period can be seen.'[19]

For the US, the fate of Cyprus was less important than its strategic value for monitoring the Soviet threat and so Britain's rights to operate through its sovereign bases by virtue of the 1960 treaties was paramount, and superseded their interest in the rivalries between Greece and Turkey. Callaghan later stated that military and 'high-level' State Department officials repeatedly asked for the intelligence bases to be saved. Under the terms of an earlier agreement, if Britain had pulled out of Cyprus, America could not have taken over the running of sovereign bases and separate spying sites inside Cypriot territory. Cyprus had 'extreme value' as a 'centre for electronic surveillance of the Soviet Union's nuclear activities, the cold war was hotting up and there were new Soviet missile test facilities being developed near the Caspian Sea, which we were able to look over. So the Americans didn't want us to go.'[20] The nuclear arms race and the ability to spy on Soviet missile deployments steered the direction of both US and British foreign policy in the region.

In the US, the new Ford Administration faced questions in Congress demanding to know what part it had played in the lead up to the invasion and subsequent events. Fierce criticism came particularly from the Greek political lobby in Washington, which successfully led a challenge to the continued sales of arms to Turkey that resulted in a partial embargo in retaliation for the use of US supplied military weapons in the invasion: in contravention of rules permitting their use only in self-defence, and yet with the express consent of the US authorities. This was viewed as an important demonstration of how the Greek–American lobby could be mobilised to influence US foreign policy although too late to change events on the ground.

Throughout this period the overriding concern for the US was in protecting its strategic interests against any form of Soviet expansion in the Eastern Mediterranean. It was always nervous that the Communist AKEL party if elected in its own right would drift closer towards Moscow's sphere of influence (ironically, this is exactly what happened a generation later, when AKEL won the presidency in 2009).[21] Their missile bases in Turkey having been withdrawn as a consequence of the covert deal struck during the Cuban Missile Crisis, the next best way to check that expansion was to have Cyprus bristling with spy facilities. Any invasion would not have changed that role in the long run. It did not ultimately matter whether parts of the island were in Greek or Turkish hands – both played their role as a proxy arm of US surveillance in the region. Indeed, there is considerable evidence from CIA and the State Department Bureau of Intelligence records to show that Washington was repeatedly warned of the Junta's intentions and Turkish preparations for a retaliatory invasion, but the State Department failed to act to stop them, as it had in the past. The significance of such records is itself a matter of intense, ongoing debate.[22] But even if no active collusion to allow the Turkish arrival took place, there was certainly no serious action to prevent or prepare for it.

US Secretary of State Henry Kissinger was reticent on the Cyprus issue for a long time. It wasn't until 1999 that he finally returned to the subject in his new book, *Years of Renewal*, under the chapter heading: 'Cyprus, a case study in ethnic conflict'. He likened the Cyprus troubles to later wars in Bosnia, Somalia, Rwanda and Chechnya; an age-old blood feud between Greeks and Turks, with the Americans simply trying to extinguish the flames before they set light to the whole of NATO's south-eastern wing. But Kissinger's account is highly selective – that of a key player with his own place in history to defend. By painting the situation as a purely ethnic conflict, Kissinger overlooks the paradox that Greece and Turkey, as well as being age-old enemies, are also allies who continuously plotted together with the aim of serving their own interests against the wishes of the Cypriots;

and he conveniently avoids addressing the responsibility that Britain and the United States must bear for contributing to the problem. He mentions the overriding need to placate Turkey as a strategic Cold War ally in the region, with their numerous spy stations and friendly military bases, but ignores, and does not even mention, the substantial Cypriot installations that served British and American interests, the spying and electronic surveillance installations in the Sovereign Bases Areas and other locations.[23]

Cyprus now entered a new very unstable phase of its history where treaty guarantees were seen as mere scraps of paper. Turkey appeared to have explored the terms of the island's founding to carve out its own proxy state, and British support had not been forthcoming to prevent this. By its actions the Greek Junta had damaged the elected government of the island, and although it played a determined role in supporting the defence of the Greek Cypriots against the Turkish invasion, its credibility and capacity to raise international support was marred by the role it had played in sparking the crisis in the first place.

It is extremely difficult to erase from the psyche of many Greek Cypriots their belief, rightly or wrongly, in a profound US culpability for failing to prevent the disastrous events of July and August 1974.[24] As an economic and humanitarian disaster it rivalled, relative to population size, the break-up of the former Yugoslavia in the nineties.

Up to 200,000 Greek Cypriots were displaced from the Northern Occupied areas. 60,000 Turkish Cypriots living in the south were transferred to the north by 1975. In terms of casualties, 4,500–6,000 killed and wounded (both military and civilian personnel) Also up to 1,600 are still reported missing, many of whom were taken prisoner to Turkish mainland prisons during and immediately after the 1974 hostilities. It is not unreasonable to compare the scale of the disaster involving the transfer of populations with the exchange of ethnicities between Greece and Turkey after the Greek–Turkish war in the 1920s.[25] Such a dramatic reversal left its stamp on the psychology of a generation of Greek Cypriot governments, and profoundly shaped the economic and political direction of the country – up to and including its presence in the eurozone, and parallel to that, the deregulated system of international finance.

There was an important change in the nature of the EU's (formerly the European Community (EC)) involvement in the Cyprus issue when Greece became a member in 1981. Greek membership meant the country would use the institutions of the EU/EC in two distinct ways: one was to prevent the recognition of Turkish Cypriots inside the EU's political and economic framework – and the second was to link all new developments between Turkey and the EU to the resolution of the Cyprus problem. One example of this leverage was reflected in the subsequent ban on Turkish Cypriots' exports to the EU states. For example, in 1976, the EU had formulated a de facto arrangement for the continuation of North Cyprus's exports to the UK and Ireland. However, Greek membership of the EU in 1981 meant that the continuation of this policy became legally impossible within the EU, and culminated in a ban on most goods from the occupied zone in July 1994.[26]

On 3th July 1990, the Greek Cypriot administration of Cyprus applied to the EU for full membership. What motivated the Greeks and Greek Cypriots was the perception that Cyprus's accession to the EU would be the catalyst for unification of the island. First, this would exert pressure on Turkey to make concessions on the Cyprus conflict in return for Turkey's membership in the EU. Second, since the Turkish forces would be regarded as occupying the territory of an EU member state, they would concede to the reunification of the island. Nonetheless, the EU expected to get its first diplomatic success by uniting the island through the membership incentives. The Commission Opinion of 1993 stated that:

> The Commission feels that a positive signal should be sent to the authorities and the people of Cyprus confirming that the Community considers Cyprus as eligible for membership and that as soon as the prospect of a settlement is surer, the Community is ready to start the process with Cyprus that should eventually lead to its accession.[27]

This seemed then a positive incentive for both sides of the conflict to resolve their differences. By 2004, it was clear they would not; but membership of the EU and eventually the eurozone would proceed regardless.

## A Final Hope? The Annan Plan, 2002–2004

The Annan Plan was a United Nations proposal to resolve the Cyprus dispute. The proposal sought to restructure the Republic of Cyprus as a 'United Republic of Cyprus', or a federation of two states. It was the most important initiative to reunite the island since it broke apart in 1974 – and the last in a long series of attempts to provide a unified political solution since the collapse of constitutional rule in 1963. A UN sponsored proposal by Secretary General Kofi Annan, it was the most comprehensive attempt to provide an enduring settlement, and invoked the principles of conflict resolution theory: introducing a series of sophisticated checks and balances to separate conflicting groups help the opposing political elites govern the country.[28] The whole edifice was thereby created to nurture the spirit of future co-operation and compromise. In particular, it had a strong eye to the nation's impending integration into the EU and potentially the eurozone. The referendum wording of the question put to the voters of each community made clear the intention to have the decision (in the affirmative) in place for the accession of Cyprus to the European Union on the 1st of May 2004.[29] It asked:

> Do you approve the Foundation Agreement with all its Annexes, as well as the constitution of the Greek Cypriot/Turkish Cypriot State and the provisions as to the laws to be in force, to bring into being a new state of affairs in which Cyprus joins the European Union united?[30]

Under the plan for the new United Cyprus Republic (UCR), most of the political power of the country would be concentrated in the hands of two new constituent states – including control of industry, healthcare, commerce, education, internal security and the administration of justice. It provided for a rotating president from between the two states, proportional representation in the public services, a continued but reduced presence of the Turkish military for up to 18 years, and eventual demilitarisation of the entire island. The schedule for the demilitarisation of the island was one of the strongest sticking points for the Greek Cypriot side, as it meant that a sword of Damocles still would hang over the process while the Turkish army remained – in reduced numbers but still remaining a possible threat. For this reason, the Greek side advocated an UN-led international peace-keeping force with an enhanced mandate should remain for a limited period of time to 'police' the island, thereby safeguarding the security of all Cypriots. This approach would help to make sure that the international community kept a watchful eye on the plan's bedding down in the post signature phase – so bringing to the fore more quickly any issues affecting its successful implementation. But past experience from the period of 1964–74 had shown the UN's role in dealing with inter-communal tensions to be difficult in the extreme.

What was crucial to the 'Plan' was to incorporate a truly working constitution, but not one which would have taken Turkish Cypriots back to their 1960 position. This meant permanent restrictions on the three freedoms of movement, settlement and property, in order not to jeopardise a Turkish Cypriot dominated constituent within a federal state. There was to be separate sovereignty of both founding states, and the security ties with the respective motherlands should be maintained. As a political union, this was one built around the imposed geopolitical redraw of 1974. Critics may say that the lack of unfettered freedom of movement is contrary to the fundamental principles of the EU, an issue presently being more broadly debated in the EU now, but not being applied in the case of Cyprus.

Constitutionally, the UCR would be a federal consociational state on the Swiss model with its cantons of regional authorities linked to a federal structure. All official appointments, including the overall president, would be by proportional representation to cut across ethnic boundaries and foster cross-community political coalitions. The Greek Cypriot side accepted, during the proximity talks preceding the first version of the Annan Plan, the principle of political equality of the Turkish Cypriot side 'not as numerical equality but as effective participation. This means that at the central level decisions are made by majority but that this majority should comprise votes of both communities.'[31]

There were still fundamental concerns on both sides. From the Greek Cypriot perspective, the strength of the powers of the constituent states diluted the effectiveness and capacity of the federal authority. The counter argument was that too much power at the centre would neutralise the authority of the two constituent states – and introduced the very tensions that eventually provoked armed intervention and a regional divide in the first place. By contrast, the Turkish Cypriot representatives originally demanded that their people enjoy a separate right of self-determination, and that they must be able to cede should they feel dominated economically or politically by the Greek Cypriot side. This demand was later dropped and not included in any version of the Annan Plan. From the start of the proximity talks in December 1999, Rauf Denktash, the representative of the Turkish Cypriots in the negotiations until 2003, continued to aim – with the support of the Turkish government – at a confederal solution based on the principle of two equal peoples, two sovereign states. The demand for a confederation was subsequently abandoned by the Turkish side, though the maximum degree of sovereignty for the 'constituent' states was maintained. Turkish delegates were however unmovable on territorial concessions and Dentkas insisted they should be limited for security reasons: 'A secure territorial basis is paramount for us because we have a smaller population and because our past suffering must never be repeated.' According to Varnarva & Faustmann, 'At a later stage of the negotiations, the Turkish military also demanded a straight border line between the two constituent states for military and strategic reasons, an allusion on two deep cavities of the Greek Cypriot constituent state into the Turkish Cypriot constituent state in the last versions of the Annan Plan'.[32]

Apart from Cypriot citizenship of the UCR, each citizen was entitled to citizenship in one of the constituent states but complex rules limited the right to seek and obtain citizenship across internal 'borders'. This was to ensure that the Turkish Cypriot constituent state maintained its built-in Turkish Cypriot majority: therefore its ethnic identity continued to be defined in the localities and local communities as much as at the state level. The effect of this was ultimately to limit the number of Greek Cypriots able to move to the north, including the hundreds of thousands who had fled from their homes thirty years earlier. The Plan reinforced and was effectively sanctioning the importation of Turkish settlers from Anatolia that transformed the demographic map of Northern Cyprus. With the exception of the conflict in the Balkans, such ethnic rebalancing has not been seen in Europe since the Second World War.

The return of property formerly owned by Greek Cypriots, or an alternative compensatory scheme, was always a central plank of any future settlement. It was estimated that they had owned 90% of the property and land in the north and no settlement could take place unless this was satisfactorily addressed. The Turkish Cypriots claimed that total restitution of property would mean the North of Cyprus could not function as a constituent state within a bi-zonal, bi-communal UCR, and instead suggested that the solution was through compensation for dispossessed former owners. The Annan plan provided for the former owners in the regions of Morphou and Famagusta to gradually receive former property in a phased process as these areas fell back into Greek Cypriot control. This was to be a phased process of between one and three and a half years provided for in the territorial adjustment programme contained in Annex V1 of the Annan Plan.[33] This would not apply to those with claims in the Kyrenia district and the Karpass peninsula which would be entirely under Turkish Cypriot control but where the only remedy was through compensation. Under the plan, land and property owned by business organisations or the Church was not recoverable.

What about rights of Turkish 'illegal' settlers from Anatolia to remain after a settlement? These were Turkish settlers transferred from Turkey to the TRNC with the specific purpose of altering the demographic map. These settlers outnumber the indigenous Turkish Cypriot population by at least 2:1. Much to the opposition of the Greek Cypriot side, the plan decided to recognise the rights of those settlers who were able to establish long term residency and only provided for the return of those with less than seven years. By far this was one of the most unpopular measures in the south, as it seemed to condone the illegal entry of most of the settlers born outside Cyprus. Many Turkish Cypriots, like Greek Cypriots, had in fact emigrated after 1974 with perhaps less than 80,000 of the pre-1974 population remaining – those people for whom the shaky legal premise of the entire invasion was founded.

These many concessions to northern political autonomy and ethnic identity made the plan far more palatable to the Turkish minority, but cost it vital Greek support. The final version of the plan (Annan V) was claimed to be drafted to deal with the fears on both sides but in the end it was only the Turkish Cypriot side that agreed to the provisions of the final terms of the referendum. The Greeks would overwhelmingly reject it.

It would be easy to criticise this apparent slant towards Turkish Cypriot concerns in the Annan Plan's foundation, but such a trade-off may have essentially been unsolvable by this point. As Glafcos Clerides in his final term as President of the Republic (1999–2004) puts it:

> What satisfies their fears is what increases our fears, and so we have this paradoxical situation that unless we can find a way in

which the fears of both communities are put at rest, it would be extremely difficult to find a solution to the Cyprus problem.[34]

Another expert commentator and scholar, Mumtaz Soysal was more strongly critical of the arbitrating role of Kofi Annan and his UN advisors as outsiders to Cypriot affairs, suggesting that 'The final version of the plan isn't a package on which the parties ever agreed. It is a mass of coercion written by aides to the UN Secretary General saying, "this meets you half way"' and then communicated to the parties...this "map of zones" is a map being presented to those who'll live there without any discussion.'[35] Observers and constitutional experts in the international community were also vocal in their concerns as to its ability to provide a comprehensive solution. Leading legal authorities criticised the terms of the Annan Plan, particularly in the operation of key government areas – the Reconciliation Commission, the Relocation Board, and the Supreme Court – as laying the seeds of instability and to friction and tensions in the future. By contrast, Mehmet Ali Talat, the Turkish Cypriot Prime Minister, was in favour of the plan, as was the new Turkish Prime Minister, Recep Tayyip Erdogan.[36] There were also strong economic reasons for the Turkish Cypriots to vote in favour. Economically the north was not in good shape and the prospect of joining the EU as part of a United Republic of Cyprus promised access to a much-needed tap of EU funds for local and regional development to grow its economy.

Whatever its apparent faults, the Annan plan was able to draw on the lessons of past negotiations to try and avoid those elements of greatest contention, namely the Turkish insistence on local autonomy in a bi-communal state. The authors had in mind the problems of the 1960 Constitution and the extensive powers of veto in the old presidential system, which could and did bring effective government to a standstill.

The new plan did not remove the problem of the veto, although it tried to integrate it into the structure of government in such a way that no one person or group could veto decisions that could paralyse the day to day business of government. A federated state with a more devolved power structure was intended to mitigate the likelihood of both legislative and executive deadlock: and on a social level, reconcile the desire of two communities both for ethnic autonomy, and the widespread benefits of a unified and peaceful island nation. Whether its architects had adequately addressed these issues is difficult to say, and with its rejection impossible to tell. Nevertheless, its achievements at garnering support were not insubstantial. The plan that received acceptance by two-thirds of the Turkish community, and was perceived as providing the basic security features for their community in a constituent state in a revised federal constitution. The 'yes' vote in the north demonstrated a fresh outlook and willingness to try and coexist. But the 'no' vote conjured up old fears that the Greeks did not want to live together in a federated state, or indeed in any state where they were not the dominant ethnic and political grouping.

Security issues cannot be overemphasised, as these are crucial to the psyche of Greek and Turkish Cypriots. For the latter, these had been largely met by the presence of an overwhelmingly powerful Turkish military force of 35,000 troops (to be scaled down over two decades under the plan) with armoured support stationed in the North as a solid guarantee of their safety.[37] There was no proportionate counterbalance of security for the Greek side, apart from a token contingent. Without the immediate removal of these troops (or at least their accelerated reduction to levels close to those permitted under the 1960 treaties), it was difficult for many Greek Cypriots to endorse the Annan Plan.

In the end it was those concerns, and the failure of the plan to adequately address them, which led to its decisive rejection by the Greek Cypriot population of the island. Exit polls held after the referendum, April 24, 2004, show that three-quarters of those Greek Cypriots who voted 'no' stated that security concerns constituted the most important reason for their rejection of the Annan Plan.[38] Nathalie Tocci, an expert on conflict resolution and a keen observer on the Cyprus issue, quotes in an article for *The International Spectator* entitled 'Reflections on Post-Referendum Cyprus', a separate poll amongst the 'no' voters revealing that for 80% of them the fear that Turkey would not deliver on its commitments was the main reason for rejecting the plan.[39] The UN Secretary General acknowledged the decisive role of the security aspect in his Report on his good offices in Cyprus after the referendum: '[...] fears regarding security and implementation appear to be prominent amongst Greek Cypriots – based, to a significant extent, on historic distrust of Turkish intentions.'[40]

There were those on the Greek side in favour of a 'yes' vote, who included two former presidents Glafcos Clerides and George Vassiliou as well as the centre right Democratic Rally opposition party. Some complained that the 'yes' case was not effectively broadcasted owing to the fact that media support was deemed to be closely linked to President Tassos Papadopoulos who was championing the 'no' vote to the Annan plan. This view was echoed by the UN itself, which also claimed that it was not able to present to the Greek Cypriot side the benefits of the 'yes' case in the period before voting day – the (controversial) allegation being that its representatives were refused access to broadcasters and press.[41]

The Annan Plan did more to raise questions than answers for the future of Cyprus. Would it create a unitary state out of the de facto situation created by the 1974 invasion and the creation of the TRNC? No, at best it establishes a confederation of two constituent states on a small island half the size of Wales. Would it deal with the human-itarian issues of displaced persons in 1974 – representing at the time 200,000 Greek Cypriots formerly resident in the north, as well over 50,000 Turkish Cypriots uprooted from their homes in the south? Not sufficiently – only a small fraction of Greek Cypriots would be permit-ted to return 'home'. Worse still, compensation for loss of properties would not come from any international backed schemes – as had been discussed in earlier years – but directly from internal Cypriot special income tax compensation funds, effectively funding repara-tions to its own citizens as a result of the 1974 invasion displacing them in the first place.[42]

Nevertheless, a profound disappointment was the main sentiment evoked in the response that was offered internationally by govern-ments, spokespeople and media pundits. Turkey's Prime Minister, Recep Tayyip Erdoğan, was able to say that the 'yes' vote in the north had put Turkish Cypriot isolation to an end.[43] The Greek gov-ernment emphasised the need for continued dialogue, a spokesman stressing that it is 'in the interest of everyone to continue efforts to reconcile Greek Cypriots and Turkish Cypriots.'[44] UN Secretary General, Kofi Annan, referred to the decision … 'A unique and his-toric chance to resolve the Cyprus problem has been missed.[45] For Britain, echoing international sentiment, the foreign secretary, Jack Straw, stated: 'We will respect the choice which Greek Cypriots have expressed today. But I hope they will continue to reflect on whether this choice is the right one for them.'[46]

For the EU, a 'yes' vote would bring the whole of the island into the EU in May 2004, although it had already been agreed that the Republic of Cyprus, having met the pre-accession arrangements in the *Acqui Communitaire*, would become a member regardless of the outcome.[47] It could be argued that the agreement to let the Republic of Cyprus join on the 1st of May 2004, irrespective of the referendum outcome, encouraged lobbying by Cypriot diplomats and politicians for a 'no' vote as a sensible, lower-risk outcome. It was felt that once inside the EU, the Greek Cypriot side would be in a better position to push their case in future negotiations for a more equitable settlement.

Echoing the view in much of the international media, *The Economist* magazine offered this opinion right before the vote, when the polls looked dire for the prospects of unification:

> What the Greek Cypriots are about to pass up may very well be their last, best chance for at least half of those displaced in 1974 to recover their homes; to bring about a massive reduction in the size of the island's Turkish garrison; and to benefit from the goodwill and assistance which a settlement would attract. If the 'no' vote is massive, then the 30-year charade of trying to solve the Cyprus conflict by reuniting the island will be over for good.[48]

That the Annan Plan marks the end of the road for all efforts at union will be disputed in chapter five of this book. *The Economist* also ignored just how poor the offer for those displaced persons actually was in the plan, or how limited the presence would be, real or potential, of the Turkish military over the island's affairs. 'Goodwill and assistance' may indeed have been forthcoming from a settlement, whatever that means in real, material terms. But For the Greek Cypriot side to have voted 'Yes' would have been an enormous leap of faith: and one which needed abundant reserves of good will to handle the many issues, complexities and concerns of the plan's implementation for years to come. The obvious retort to this point is that the Turkish side willingly embraced these challenges. But the north had the full might of the Turkish army to protect them, should things turn sour – just as they had a generation earlier.

Studies have been conducted to provide also a psychological analysis of the Greek Cypriot 'no' vote. One carried out at the University of Cyprus in 2006 examined two characteristic fears it defined as *Realistic* and *Symbolic*. *Realistic* fear centred on security and economic issues: such as how a settlement may affect standards of living, the effect on the economy and security. Fear remained, in particular, that inter-communal strife would return and possibly lead to Turkish military action, even down below the 'green line', which marked the point where invasion forces halted in August 1974. Geographically, Greece was too far away to prevent invasion. Turkish Jets could operate with impunity in Cypriot airspace, as they had decades earlier. The nearest Turkish airbase was less than 60 miles away, whereas the nearest in Greece was from the island of Crete, over 400 miles distant.

*Symbolic* fears were to be defined as more of those relating to threats to Greek values, culture, heritage and religious beliefs and how these may be threatened in the new state of affairs. These were fears which were deeper, more abstract, less substantial: they were not strictly grounded in specific, rational concerns, but more the result of a generational siege mentality created by the invasion and partition. These were shown in the study, and other writings, to play a substantial role in underpinning the more concrete concerns of the plan. As one author put it, 'The rejection of the Annan Plan was a psychological expression as well. It was the manifestation of fear (or phobia) against something that was perceived as a threat.' Thirty years of uneasy peace had not erased the scars of conflict – whether military or inter-communal.[49] Moreover, the overriding threat to the future of Cyprus lies in the continuing presence of Turkish armed forces in the North which does not contribute to a viable solution to its future stability. In essence, the main obstacle to a comprehensive settlement to the security problem lies in Turkey's strategic interests, made more poignant by the importance of the shipping lanes below its southern coasts and the energy discoveries in the various quadrants around the shores of Cyprus promising future wealth for the island.

Since 1993, the European Commission, member states and the Republic of Cyprus itself had raised the expectation that the prospect of Cyprus' EU membership would act as a catalyst for a settlement of the island's conflict. Yet the divisions between the positions of the principal parties widened and the 1990s witnessed an escalation of tensions in the Eastern Mediterranean. By 2004, it was clear that the peace process for this generation had failed. Yet this did not stop a divided island from joining the EU shortly after, and the eurozone four years later.

The EU will not have forgotten that Greek Cypriots – whatever the merits of that decision – voted overwhelmingly against the Annan Plan to end the longstanding political conflict, at least in its current form. But the fact is the de jure Republic of Cyprus was still able to join the EU as Brussels had not imposed any precondition for a constitutional settlement. It should be noted that many of the concerns highlighted by Greek Cypriots, in this study and other polls, saw profound economic concerns about Greeks and Turks living side by side in a United Cyprus Republic. High unemployment, lower wages, and economic instability that could catalyse widespread social unrest were all key to people's fears. Few dreamt that this scenario would rapidly come to pass without that political union – but came about following a very different kind of integration, that of Cyprus with the eurozone.

# 3
# The Financial Crisis Spreads to Cyprus

## The Single Currency and International Finance

The collapse of the Cypriot banking system has to be seen in the context of the global economic downturn, which was triggered by the US subprime mortgage crisis of 2007–8 but had its origins in the macroeconomic policies of at least the past decade. A broad-based consumer boom coupled with ultra-loose monetary policy by central banks in the US and Europe fed a global speculative bubble in real estate and equity markets. The fallout of this gigantic credit bust took its time to unwind across the eurozone; emerging as an ongoing sovereign debt crisis that owes its origin as much to the structural problems of the single currency, and state spending in the eurozone, as it does to banking leverage, global finance, and the securitisation of toxic debt. Cyprus itself saw the worst of its effects comparatively late – until 2012, in fact, it had appeared to weather the global recession remarkably well. What makes the story of this island somewhat different is the extent to which the causes of the crisis were reaped *after*, rather than before, the global bubble burst in 2007–8. In this light, the island marks a new phase in the evolving dilemma of the eurozone – one bound up in the problems and processes of how the region has struggled to adapt to the world after the financial crisis; and the difficult and fraught consequences of its various bailouts, austerity plans, and monetary policy solutions.

On January 1, 2008, Cyprus joined the eurozone. This event was the culmination of decades of effort to bring the island, isolated by its geography and divided by recent war, closer to the heart of Europe:

with corresponding straight access to European capital. Both admission into the European Union in 2004, and entry into the single currency four years later, were intended to enhance the political and financial clout of the island, to provide a greater guarantee on its contracted borders, and to enjoy the stabilising benefits of the single currency. The process of integration went hand in hand with the development of the country as a centre of international finance.

Entry into the single currency marked the pivot point in the financial, economic, and social history of the island. It fastened her fate securely to the hazy and tumultuous fortunes of the eurozone, its currency and debt markets, and the Troika committee of institutions. It also helped feed a credit bubble on a scale the island was not prepared for, and had never seen. Eurozone interest rates were kept deliberately low by the European Central Bank, and the rampant increase in the availability of easy credit made readily available by the banks helped to fuel the accelerated drive in consumer spending. A source close to the government, who wishes to remain anonymous, puts it that: 'When credit was very easily available and bank lending had already got out of control, it was the massive credit expansion unparalleled in the EU which fuelled the property boom.'[1] Banks' loan books expanded almost a third in 2008 as its newly earned eurozone status made Cyprus a more attractive destination for banking and business generally – though Cypriot banks maintained the unusual position of funding almost all their lending from deposits (with even home loans typically requiring a 30% down payment, over double the EU average). 'When Cyprus joined the single European currency, Greek and other euro area deposits were reclassified as domestic, leading to billions more local lending,' a prominent member of Cyprus' House of Representatives remarked, retrospectively, at the height of the 2013 crisis.[2]

The advantages offered by the small nation were numerous. Cyprus has a legal system based on English law, that follows English accounting rules: and buttressed by an unusually high concentration of lawyers and accountants. The strength of this post-imperial arrangement means that numerous foreign interests, especially Russian, have corporations based in Cyprus, and organise their global business from the island. This model is not dissimilar to what exists in other highly developed eurozone states with highly leveraged banking sectors – for example, the Netherlands and Luxembourg – though their domestic banks are not the ones so heavily exposed. In Luxembourg in particular, the vast bank deposits held are almost entirely by foreign banks.

Cyprus offered savings rates which could not be matched. A depositor would have earned €300,000 interest on a €1 million deposit held for the last five years in Cyprus, compared to the €150,000 to €180,000 the same deposit would have made in Italy and Spain, and the mere €80,000 interest it would have accrued in Germany. The island became a financial nexus without a financial district: a hub for huge flows of capital without the trappings of distinction that dominate the cityscapes of London, Frankfurt, New York and Zurich. Many of those depositors happened to be Russians; Cyprus, as much as London, was a playground for ex-Soviet business tycoons because of low dividend taxes and the use of business-friendly English law. Major Russian businesses are owned, in whole or part, by Cypriot holding companies. Moody's, the credit ratings agency, estimated in 2013 that Russian banks had $12 billion and private individuals another $19 billion on deposit with banks in Cyprus.[3]

The proportionate scale of this foreign influx of deposits is made clear in the Troika-mandated advisor, the Pacific Management Investment Company's (PIMCO) due diligence report on the Cyprus banking system from February 2013:

> As of June 2012, the banking system was primarily deposit-funded with 71% of liabilities composed of deposits. Of these deposits, only 40% are from Cypriot residents according to data submitted by PIs. Of the remaining total, 34% come from non-residents that operate in Cyprus in part due to the current system of tax and business incentives, 19% from Greece and 7% from other countries. With respect to loans, 62% of loans were reported in Cyprus with 29% in Greece and 9% in other countries.[4]

From this, the report highlights 'the degree to which domestic lending activity and international expansion have been funded by non-resident deposits.'[5] The result of this was 'dramatic' growth in the sector. Total assets of the Cyprus banking sector stood at €143 billion as of 31 March, 2012. As a result of this growth in total assets – along with lending standards that generally focused much more on the collateral of a loan than on the borrowers' debt service capacity –

Cyprus private sector credit as share of GDP rose to one of the highest levels of any economy on record according to World Bank data. And the report continues: 'Access to external funding also helped to fuel an external expansion on the part of the Cyprus banks, primarily in Greece, but to a lesser extent in the UK, Russia and other Eastern European countries.' Consequently, 'While some of this diversification into international units has helped to offset the emerging problems at the core Cyprus banking operations, the expansion into Greece has been a source of significant strain for the Cyprus banks operating there.'⁶ A financial expert who wishes to remain anonymous puts the point across more bluntly, saying that the banks 'had no diversification in their portfolios and invested heavily in Greek bonds.'

The prevalence of asset-based lending practices, particularly in regard to the property market, led to a further brewing problem, as it leveraged such loans against the continuing rise in property prices. Cypriot banks lent out money only if the borrower had some strong collateral to back their loan (in most cases real estate), with less attention given to whether the client had the ability to actually *meet* payments through their income and earnings. There was a certain logic to this process: if the borrowers got into trouble, they could always sell their property to repay their loans; and as real estate prices increased for a very long time, this practice rarely yielded losses for the banks. Most importantly, borrowers who were not able to repay could always pledge more collateral and actually increase the amount they borrowed. This, in turn, artificially increased the size of loans, leading to the concentration of bad loans to fewer business and financial entities: and leveraging its stability (like so much ultimately bad lending in the United States before 2008) on the continued (and unsustainable) rising fortunes of the property market. Because this approach deprioritises the ability of the borrower to directly pay from income, an apparent strength of this system was also a hidden weakness – one that took longer than the early days of the recession to become truly apparent. PIMCO appears to have stumbled on this realisation, for as they observe:

> The relative inattention paid at origination to borrowers' ability to service their loans has resulted in a sharp response to deteriorating economic conditions in the form of heightened serious

delinquency ratios. Indeed, *the marginal response of loan performance to changes in economic conditions appears much greater in
Cyprus than in many other economies.* This attention to collateral
and relative inattention to debt service capacity helps to explain
why non-performing loan ratios in Cyprus are so elevated despite
recent economic performance that has been more robust than that
seen in more economically distressed European countries.[7]

Similarly, the 2013 Memorandum of Understanding (MoU) report
on the island noted this internal element, though it does not (rightly
so) assign it sole or primary cause:

> The banking sector has been severely affected by the broader
> European economic and sovereign crisis, in particular through its
> exposure to Greece. However, many of the sector's problems are
> home-grown and relate to overexpansion in the property market
> as a consequence of banks' poor risk management practices.[8]

Entry into the eurozone may have stimulated an explosion in
financial activity, but it does not mark the beginning of the trend.
A senior source in the banking sector, who wishes to remain anonymous, refers to how 'this five year term was marked by their mission
for Cyprus – to the EU in 2004, and to the Eurozone in 2008... The
term marked a very rapid growth in the economy' but with 'little
foresight of the real estate sector' and with 'little or few measures
were taken to contain its overheating'. For this, they say that both
the government and banks 'have their share of responsibility'. The
Tax Amnesty granted by the Tassos Papadopoulos government for
the period of 2004–2008 attracted a flood of tax flight funds from
around Europe – or what one EU source describes as an 'amnesty
of capital influence in Cyprus'.[9] By its own terms, the policy was a
roaring success – it attracted increased receipts estimated to reach CY
£110 million by mid-February 2005: more than double the anticipated amount of £50 million.[10] This move was coupled with the
attractive interest rates for all expats and foreign depositors, especially Russians, and flooded the banks with new liquidity. Much of
this was used to provide loans which fuelled a housing bubble rather
than supporting the primary drivers of lasting growth, such as export
goods and SMEs.[11]

Bulging deposit books not only fuelled a credit expansion at home, but also drove Cypriot banks overseas: with Greece the destination *par excellence* for the island's two biggest lenders, Laiki and the Bank of Cyprus. The close cultural, military, spiritual and ancestral ties between Greece and Cyprus meant the Cypriot banks did not easily heed caution about this level of exposure. The banks sold down some of their Greek holdings, but then got back into the market as yields rose – including even in 2011, when German banks were offloading Greek debt as fast as possible.

The rapid expansion produced a banking sector that was eight times the size of the nation's gross domestic output – a fact assorted European ministers would eagerly line up to criticise a few years later in 2013, during the bailout talks. Ironically, when Cyprus was being considered for membership of the European Union in 2003, a European Commission report mentioned no problems, real or potential, in its banking sector. Nor did the European Central Bank (ECB), or indeed the International Monetary Fund (IMF), mention anything wrong with Cypriot banks or their business model when it evaluated whether the country was fit to join the eurozone in a 2007 report. No real red flags were raised by any of these institutions until as late as 2012. 'The banks were considered super conservative,' said Alexander Apostolides, an economic historian at Cyprus' European University, a private university on the outskirts of Nicosia.[12]

Whatever the motives behind both the expansion and its limited oversight, the exposure to Greek debt defied sovereign risk standards typically applied by central banks; a clause in Cyprus' EU/IMF December Memorandum of Understanding explicitly requires the banks to have more diversified portfolios of higher credit quality. 'That [the way the exposures were allowed to build] was a problem of supervision,' said Papageorgiou, a member of the six-man board of directors of the central bank at the time. Michael Sarris, the (then) Minister of Finance, also described Laiki as 'a successful bank that took the wrong direction after 2006.'[13]

Whatever toxic financial concoction was being brewed in this new business world, it took time and a new, more deadly European debt climate for its effects to show. The global crisis hit the shores of Cyprus only after a substantial time lag, and its impact appeared remarkably muted. GDP growth slowed from 4.4% in 2007 to 3.7% in 2008 – but this was at a time when the global economy was already in recession. The Cypriot economy itself fell into recession in 2009 with its economy shrinking by 1.67% – its first year of negative economic growth since the Turkish invasion.[14] The fallout hit the economy hardest in its traditional flagship industries, namely tourism and shipping. But the island's recession was less severe than many expected. It was a fraction of what was experienced in much of the western world – with the US economy shrinking 5.1% from peak to trough in 2007–9[15] – and the 5.5% felt by Cyprus itself in the crisis of 2013. Such a fate appears, at least on the surface, to be precisely the opposite of that faced by the other notoriously financialised island, Iceland, whose economy had already imploded by the end of 2008. Unemployment increased significantly, from 3.7% in 2008 to 6.3% in 2008, with youth unemployment particularly high. But the majority of this was only of a short duration of less than one year.[16]

There are several reasons why the island at least appeared to have weathered the global storm in good order. Compared with Portugal, Ireland, Greece and Spain ('PIGS'), public debt had been well contained, both during the boom years and at least the onset of the crisis. The centre-right government of Tassos Papadopoulos ended 2007 with a 3.3% surplus, and the island's debt-to-GDP ratio had fallen to just 49% by the end of 2008, compared with 70% for the eurozone as a whole, and 170% in Greece.[17] Overheated housing prices meant that the commercial and retail property market fell 30% from their 2007 peak. However, unlike in Spain, Ireland and the UK – all of which experienced a comparable property bust – the introduction of tight loan-to-value ratios before Cyprus entered the eurozone helped contain the risks associated with the rapid rise of the real estate sector.[18] Indeed, Cypriot banks typically demanded a down payment of 30 per cent for home loans, well above the average in most developed countries. When Lehman Brothers collapsed in late summer 2008, most of the world's banks suffered in the fallout, but not, it appeared, Cyprus's.

Yet within four years of the formal end of the Great Recession, the Cypriot economy was in free fall, public debt had exploded, government bonds were reduced to junk status, and the financial system was on its knees. By March 2013, the bail-in proposal by the Troika meant that euro deposits in Cyprus had become inferior to euro deposits held elsewhere: an event in singular defiance of every modern standard of international banking, to say nothing of the entire principle of a common single currency.

The causes of this apparent transformation of national fortune are complex. In the ideologically heated climate of introspection that followed the 2013 bailout, criticism has been levied at policies past and present, from both Left and Right, and against targets as varied as different Cypriot governments, the IMF and the eurozone as a whole. In particular, the question of how far the seeds for the crisis were laid in the policies of the previous administration is a matter for which many conflicting views can be cited; and, consequently, competing agendas of authorship need to be carefully considered.

It bears noting at this stage, however, just how little foresight the IMF and European Commission at least publically had about the vulnerabilities of the banking sector there, especially as the debt crisis in Greece and round the eurozone mounted. In a 2010 report by one of the EU Commission's key advisory bodies – its proclaimed 'expert network',[19] the ASISP (Analytical Support on the Socio-Economic Impact of Environmental Protection Reforms) – entitled 'Pensions, Health and Long-Term Care', the Cypriot financial sector was described as relatively safe from the impact of the global crisis, as 'the comparatively low degree of internationalisation of its banking system, and limited exposure to toxic assets that triggered off the credit crunch.'[20] Apparently a financial system built on international capital flows and reaching eight times GDP, with a heavy exposure in troubled bonds, qualified for the words 'low' and 'limited' here. The IMF appears to have taken an even more nonchalant approach to the situation on the island, with this rather astonishing assessment offered as late as February 2011:

> The Cypriot banking system has weathered the economic difficulties well and appears to be in sound overall condition. It has benefitted from reliance on deposits rather than less stable sources of financing, conservative lending practices, close attention to capital and liquidity buffers, and vigilant supervision. These factors have helped shield the banking system from the pressures that are prevalent in many other countries.[21]

## AKEL: An Easy Target for Blame?

More attention was stoked up by political developments on the island. In February 2008, the Cypriot public voted the leader of the AKEL party – or the Progressive Party of Working People – as President of the Republic.[22] Although AKEL had governed in coalition before, this was the first time it received enough votes to establish a nominally 'Communist' government in the island's short parliamentary history since independence. This also made them the first and only ruling Communist party in Europe since the fall of the Berlin Wall – and the only one to ever be a part of the EU.

It is not surprising that this has made it an easy target for extensive and sometimes exultant criticism, in the light of what has unfolded since 2008. While a fair share of blame can be pointed in this direction, it must be pointed out that many of the processes internal to Cyprus that were involved in the crisis were already well developed before the AKEL government took office in 2008 – to say nothing of those external and international in origin. That said, it must be noted that, politically, Cyprus operates a top-down heavy system of government in which the executive branch is effectively in the near-absolute control of the president; without the same extensive parliamentary and legislative powers of scrutiny and veto found in countries such as Great Britain or the United States. Such a system leaves substantial powers concentrated in the hands of the ruling party, and therefore grants individual administrations a wide scope for implementing their agendas.

AKEL ran at a time of apparent economic and financial prosperity, with a platform to both substantially improve the welfare system, and tackle the political divisions that had now plagued the island since 1974. The years after 2008 therefore witnessed an explosion in social spending, with increases in real terms of 15% in 2008, 11% in 2009, and 12% in 2010. These rapid increases were hailed by the government as a pivotal achievement in reforming the social condition of the island. Much of the expenditure went on an expansion of the state sector, with the number of government employees increasing by 9% from the fourth quarter of 2007 to 2010. A total of 1.2 billion euros was spent on welfare in the same time period, with benefits increasing over 2008 alone by 30%.[23] Low-income pensions also increased from 9% to 16%.[24]

Whatever the well-intentioned benefits of such welfare reforms, no significant steps appear to have been taken to ensure the funding of these provisions. The European Commission noted the difficulty Cyprus would face in meeting its projected increase in expenditures to meet its ageing-related obligations. As it said in 2010:

> Despite fiscal strains, in 2009 social spending increased in order to cushion the effects of the crisis. Particularly important has been the implementation of the Social Support Scheme for Low-Income Pensioners since December 2009, as a means of addressing the steadily high poverty rates among elderly people.

The consequence of all this additional spending was that:

> Sustainability of pensions has been an issue of public concern over the last few years... These constitute a major issue of public debate particularly as rapidly increasing pension expenditure for civil service retirees exerts strains on the rather high fiscal deficit. The Stability and Growth Plan recently submitted to the European Commission strongly stresses the need for reducing costs in respect to the state payroll and pensions expenditure.[25]

The Central Bank of Cyprus (CBC) also raised concerns. In a letter addressed to the President in December 2009, the CBC, under the leadership of then Governor Athanasios Orphanides, offered a warning about the deteriorating fiscal condition of the nation, stating: 'The situation is critical. It is imperative that a medium-term strategic plan for fiscal correction be developed... the sooner the appropriate measures are taken, the milder the consequences will be.' This was followed by a starker, more urgent message in May 2010 that drew attention to the visibly worsening situation in Greece:

> The recent dramatic events in Greece have intensified existing concerns about Cyprus... This has put fiscal problems elsewhere under the microscope... Cyprus has not yet attracted close scrutiny because of its small size. In my view, this is just a matter of time... [because of] the worsening fiscal deficits and high level of public and private debt... the very large size of the banking sector compared to GDP... I stress that unless there is a change of

direction with meaningful fiscal consolidation, primarily on the expenditure side, the consequences for the Cypriot economy will be catastrophic.[26]

'We are on the verge of economic collapse,' said Ioannis Kasoulides, the island's former foreign minister, more bluntly, 'unless serious structural reforms are implemented.'[27]

One can easily make the argument that AKEL came in at the coincidentally worst possible time for its type of aggressive social democratic spending plans to be fiscally viable. The economy of Europe, Cyprus and indeed the world in February 2008 was quite different from that of a year or two later. Even apparently strong economies fell into recession in this period: and the island's fortunes, both as a eurozone nation and a hub for global capital, were acutely sensitive to these kinds of international variables.

Nevertheless, little appears to have been done to adjust for changing circumstances, and the above warnings had no visible impact. Consequently, an economy that stagnated with the global downturn, coupled with accelerated government spending, led to a rapid deterioration in public finances. As Sarris describes it, 'We allowed public finances to deteriorate very quickly between 2007 and 2009. We had almost a 10% of GDP turnaround... That by any standards is silly.' Such a slide, with public debt rising from 49% to 70% within two years, impacted international confidence, as 'markets were already very sensitive to rapid changes in the debt of the country. It did not matter if the debt was below the average of the EU, what mattered was that it was getting worse in a hurry.'[28] This culminated in their expulsion from capital markets:

No one was willing to lend us money in April/May 2011 because they saw the problems in the banking sector and the problems... [in] government, so they feared that there was no support that could be given to the banking system. The credit agencies pointed out that if you have problems in your banking systems, how could you support it? They didn't have the funds... so we were excluded from the market in April 2011 and unfortunately we chose to stay out of the markets for the next three years, which was suicide. No other country in the world has stayed out of the capital markets for so long.

One senior source, who wishes to remain anonymous, suggests that the 'alarms' raised by the behaviour of the government provoked the disappearance of depositors funds from the banking system: 'We started seeing flight of capital, small in the beginning but continually increasing as long as the government did nothing to provide security, and instability increased,' meaning that 'by 2013...nearly half the deposits of Laiki had left the system.' Yet at the same time '...the government failed to take any action. Instead of decreasing...the national debt kept increasing at twice the speed that revenue was increasing', turning a surplus of 3% to a deficit of 6% by the end of 2010.[29] Such capital flight was only to exacerbate the disastrous impact of the Greek 'Private Sector Initiative' a year later.

The enormous rise in state spending was not the only factor that affected government finances in this period. The Evangelos Florakis Naval Base explosion that occurred on July 11, 2011, was the worst peacetime military accident ever recorded in Cyprus. In terms of artificial, non-nuclear explosions, the incident was the 4th largest accidental event in the world, and the 7th largest overall. It occurred after containers of explosives – confiscated by the US Navy from a Russian-owned Iranian ship travelling to Syria in 2009 – were left in high temperatures on the Florakis Naval Base near the island's biggest power plant; destroying it and inflicting an immediate energy crisis, as well as widespread local damage. At the time of the incident, it appears they had been left out in the open for two years.[30]

The resulting explosion killed 13 people, 12 of them immediately, including Captain Andreas Ioannides, the Commander of the Navy (Cyprus' most senior naval officer), and the base commander, Lambros Lambrou. An additional 62 people were injured. The explosion severely damaged hundreds of nearby buildings including all of the buildings in the nearby town of Zygi, and Vasilikos, the island's largest power station. As a result of the damage to the plant, the electricity supply to half the island was cut off. Rolling blackouts were instituted to conserve supplies. The electricity authority stated that 'airports, hospitals, tourist areas and industrial estates will not be affected from the power cuts in an effort not to cause problems for our economy.'[31] Nevertheless, the damage inflicted was substantial. The EU estimated that the cost of explosion to the island could amount to US$2.83bn, with cost of the power plant itself coming to US$992m. The cost of the naval disaster was, in terms of

GDP, greater than anything that any other eurozone country had to bear. The strain on public finances prompted central bank governor Orphanides to publically caution that the country may be forced to seek a bailout if planned spending cuts were not implemented fast.[32]

On October 3, 2011, Polys Polyviou, the independent state-appointed investigator charged to look into potential responsibility by state and other officials leading to the July 11 blast, released 643-page document detailing his findings of the investigation, concluding that Cypriot president Dimitris Christofias was primarily to blame for the events that led to the explosion: with both an institutional and a serious personal responsibility for the disaster.[33] The president replied with a statement in response where he 'categorically denied' any blame for the tragedy.[34] Downgrading the economy by two notches, from A2 to Baa1, Moody's said that the 'material damage' cut the country's growth trajectory from 1.8% to zero over the next year, and 'amplified' its fiscal problems.[35] Given that this was an unforeseen disaster – albeit very likely an avoidable one – an opportunity existed to apply for EU relief aid at that time or soon after, when the Governor of the Central Bank, Athanasios Orphanides, was warning that Cyprus may have to seek an EU bailout if austerity measures and increased spending cuts were not addressed.[36] Nothing was done in this regard, and the economic damage of the explosion – unalleviated by any foreign aid – proved profound.

## Greece, the PSI, and Sacrifice of Cyprus

By this time, international attention was being rapidly drawn to Greece, the weakest link in a brittle chain of eurozone economies. Greece had been living beyond its means even before it joined the euro. The country was only allowed to join the euro by blatant misaccounting that hid the equivalent of €10 billion in debt. In a now notorious financial manoeuvre, Goldman Sachs helped the country obscurify the true extent of its debt – limited by Maastricht treaty rules to 60% of GDP, and a 3% deficit – through a credit swap scheme that engineered a public deficit within the maximum entry criteria.[37] But after the country joined the single currency, public spending soared. Wages in the public sector rose over 50% between 1999 and 2008. Around €10 billion was consumed by the 2004 Olympic Games in Athens. As money flowed out of government coffers, so revenues were also hit by an endemic culture of tax evasion on an extraordinary scale; one that is estimated by the Organisation for Economic and Co-operation and Development (OECD) to account for at least €20 billion in lost revenues each year – sums that have given it the unwelcome reputation of a national pastime.[38]

The Greek economy had grown steadily throughout most of the 2000s in an apparent economic boom, but the financial crisis meant the gaping hole in the country's budget could no longer be contained – or concealed. In January 2010, the European statistics agency, Eurostat, issued a report on the debt statistics of the Greek government, pointing to 'severe irregularities' and 'institutional weaknesses' in the way the data had been collected, and suggested there had been political interference in the process.[39]

A month later, the government of George Papandreou (elected October 2009) admitted a flawed statistical procedure had existed. In April, the deficit was raised from a prior estimate of 6–8% to 13.6% of GDP – the second highest in the world behind Iceland.[40] This move rang alarm bells in international markets. Greek bonds began their rapid slide to junk status as yields soared, and US and European stock indices plunged as a Greek default and widespread debt contagion appeared to be drawing near.[41]

The Greek sovereign debt crisis has required multiple controversial bailouts, austerity measures so extreme they have caused mass riots on the streets, and tense games of political negotiation around the eurozone. The muddled and complicated steps toward its resolution have informed national, federal and monetary policy around the eurozone, and came to dramatically impact the financial fortunes of Cyprus.

On May 2, 2010, the International Monetary Fund (IMF) and a partnership of eurozone nations – with Germany heading the negotiations – agreed to a three-year, €110 billion loan, at an interest rate of 5.5% – relatively high, but far lower than the spiralling value of bond yields. Such a loan was conditional on the imposition of an austerity package without precedent in the tough nature of its terms. To make the mounting Greek debt pile sustainable, it included €30 billion of additional cuts over three years, and the privatisation of €50 billion of state assets; including the near-monopoly telecom and electricity operators, the country's two main ports in Piraeus and Thessaloniki, several small islands, and its best-capitalised financial

asset, Hellenic Postbank. Poul Thomsen, who headed the IMF nego-
tiating mission to Athens, stated in defence of these measures that,
'The alternative would be much worse for the Greek people and the
Greek leaders know that.'[42]

The Greek public was rather unimpressed by this logic, and the
austerity package was met by massive protests, civil unrest, and a
national strike.[43] With ratings agencies such as Moody's and Standard
and Poor's immediately downgrading Greek government bonds even
further down the definition of 'junk', the ECB announced on May 3
in an unprecedented offer of support that it would accept as collateral all debt instruments, new and outstanding, that were guaranteed
by the Greek government; suspending the minimum credit-rating
threshold for all such debt in an effort to maintain the solvency of
its banks.[44] Such a pro-active shift in policy came from an institution
otherwise grounded in draconian monetarist principles.

Despite the overwhelming international attention devoted to the
ills of its larger Grecian neighbour, Cyprus did not go entirely unno-
ticed in this phase of the debt crisis. A letter by the ECB to the
president in December 2010 points out a rising concern about the
fiscal condition of the island:

> In light of recent market concerns about public debt sustainability,
> it is more important than ever that every country benefiting from
> the common currency takes prompt and effective steps to ensure
> that its public finances are on a sound footing...

The letter further noted that

> Although Cyprus' sovereign debt market has a limited size, sig-
> nificant concerns exist. These concerns are particularly relevant
> in view of the large size of the Cypriot banking system, which
> may produce negative feedback loops between the financial sector
> and public debt... The challenges faced by the Cypriot economy
> require prompt corrective action.

While the bailout by the Troika had saved the Greek government
from an impending default, it did not salvage the situation for long.
By May 2011, it was evident that the economic crisis in Greece had
become so severe that the country would be unable to meet its fiscal

goals even for the prior aid package. A bilateral EU–IMF audit in June, which called for even more cuts, provoked Standard and Poor's downgrade of Greece's sovereign debt rating to CCC, the very lowest in the world, and making a default or debt write-down appear inevitable.[45] With major stock exchanges round the world consequently reeling, in July an extraordinary summit of EU leaders in Brussels extended the Greek loan repayment schedule – which they also extended to the Irish and Portuguese – from seven years to fifteen, cut the interest rate to 3.5%, and approved the construction of a new €109 billion aid package from the IMF to manage the 'exceptional and unique situation of Greece'. All EU area member states not under special assistance programmes were also required to reduce their deficits to less than 3% by 2013.[46]

The situation did not improve under these terms. The brutal recession being endured by Greece, which steadily intensified under the austerity programme, made its mounting debt pile harder to pay – and not easier in the way the bailout agreements had intended. A 2009 recession of -3.1% was followed by a -4.9% dip in 2010, and a -7.1% collapse in 2011 – numbers exceeded only by Libya and Yemen.[47] Kevin Featherstone, director of the Hellenic Observatory at the European Institute, would go on to make this observation:

> The problem is in how Greece is being rescued. The bailouts have increasingly shifted to the imposition of severe cuts across the board...Almost half of Greece's young people are unemployed, as are one in five of their older peers. Despondency is everywhere, despite the 'rescue'. If future Greek governments keep to the terms of the bailout, by 2020 public debt will be back to what is was when the crisis erupted in 2009.[48]

Unsurprisingly, over 100,000 people took to the streets against these measures in front of the Parliament building on May 29. Greek debt continued to rise and in the summer of 2011 peaked at €340 billion. In the wake of this spiral, and increased talk of a 'Grexit', or Greek exit from the eurozone, it became impossible to salvage the country's finances without a substantial 'haircut' to the value of its bonds – the oft-used wording for what was nothing less than a default on a large portion of future payments.

On October 26, 2011, with European equities in bear market territory, eurozone leaders and the IMF came to an agreement with principal European banks to accept a 50% write-off of 'notional Greek debt held by private investors' – the equivalent of €100 billion – while also guaranteeing an additional €100 billion in a multi-financing programme by the EU and IMF.[49] This PSI (Private Sector Involvement) or debt-restructuring deal was ratified by the Eurogroup in February 2012, with the European System of Central Banks (ESCB) agreeing to buy Greek bonds at this debased rate until 2020. At that point, with the debt crisis still spiralling, the European Union Council abandoned its earlier decision in favour of a more severe plan – one that was initially 50%, but went on to reach 76% of the value of holdings of Greek sovereign debt. The plan also called for an increased Core Tier One capital requirement of 9%, coupled with elevated capital buffers to be put in place by June 2012. Private investors and financial institutions were also forced to accept an additional devaluation of 53.5% on the face value of Greek government bonds, which added to the haircut in October brought the overall loss to just over 75%. This decision required, and received, the unanimous agreement of all eurozone governments, including that of the Cyprus Republic.

The biggest sovereign-debt restructuring deal in history culminated in Greece wiping some €100 billion in debt off its books. It effectively asked – or rather compelled – private bondholders to forgive bad debt on a scale never before seen by a sovereign nation. Holders of €177 billion of the €206 billion of PSI-eligible debt securities, totalling 83.5% of the bondholders, signed up to the deal.[50] Banks and large pension funds fell meekly in line. Those who did not respond to the bond-exchange offer, or the holders of around €9 billion of bonds – mostly hedge funds – which actively opposed it, were forced to accept these terms.

Whether this arrangement constituted a debt 'default' in the technical sense is a matter of debate. Technically, the nation never missed a bond payment – but this achievement may be a purely semantic one. The final terms of the deal forced a 75% haircut on its creditors, an event factored in by Standard and Poor's when they downgraded Greece's sovereign credit rating to 'selective default', the first eurozone country in its thirteen-year history to receive such a rating.[51] The International Swaps and Derivatives Association (ISDA), a collection of large financial institutions, euphemistically described

Greece's debt deal as a 'credit event', triggering payouts on credit default swap (CDS) contracts associated with a Greek default.[52] But, whatever the outside world would call it, panic did not ensue. French, German and American banks that held Greek debt did not topple; markets did not crash; contagion did not spread. Yields on troubled sovereign debtors, such as Spain and Italy, ticked up only slightly. The CDS trigger that resulted from a technical default of Greece at least appeared to be a non-event.

Yet the consequences of the Greek bailout for the management of the eurozone were substantial. As debt levels mounted, the recession deepened and the crisis magnified, the Troika became willing to go to more extreme lengths to contain the malaise. The trajectory of the measures taken became ever more aggressive; first in progressively deeper austerity cuts and enforced privatisations, and finally in the expansion of these programmes to include a direct loss to private bondholders in what was a barely disguised payment default. Each of these steps created its own new set of problems for the eurozone. Seen in the context of this trend, the 'bail-in' of Cyprus looks less like a special, unrepeatable scenario, and more the next natural step along this increasingly radical path of debt containment.

At least one member of the Troika noted the dangers of the path taken here. In a relatively frank internal report released in June 2013 – only after its contents were leaked and reported by the *Wall Street Journal* – the IMF admitted to major mistakes in its handling of the bailout of Greece; arguing that it bent the rules on its criteria for debt sustainability; underestimated the damage its prescriptions of austerity would inflict on the economy; and made overly optimistic projections on the Greek recovery.[53, 54] On the latter point, the report acknowledged that 'there were...notable failures. Market confidence was not restored, the banking system lost 30% of its deposits, and the economy encountered a much-deeper-than-expected recession with exceptionally high unemployment.'[55] It also acknowledged the possibility that 'there is a habitual tendency of Fund programs to be over-optimistic on growth until the economy reaches a bottom (and thereafter to underestimate the recovery)' and at least partly underestimated the impact of fiscal shock.[56]

Regarding the debt management programmes of 2010–2012, the report noted several problems posed by the approach taken: that the Troika arrangement was an entirely novel one in 2010; that public debt was still expected to rise, particular under the fixed-exchange rate imposed by the euro; and, most controversially, that 'the programme required the IMF's rules for exceptional access to be modified', with the criteria of 'a high probability that public debt is sustainable in the medium term' being essentially abandoned. The result of this was 'even with implementation of agreed policies, uncertainties were so significant that staff was unable to vouch that public debt was sustainable with high probability.'[57] A point to be added is the near impossibility of a country supporting such a high debt ratio without undergoing an actual economic depression. Doubts about the effectiveness of austerity measures, or the Greek ability to implement them, were exacerbated by a leaked report from the European Commission, which suggested that without substantial additional aid from as early as 2015, Greek debt could remain at 160% of GDP by 2020.[58]

Essentially the IMF changed its rules to allow countries to get 'exceptional access' to its credit lines. Its actions on the grounds of the extremity of the crisis and the domino threat posed to the eurozone by a Greek debt default: 'Given the dangers of contagion, the Fund judges the programme to have been a necessity, even though the IMF had misgivings about debt sustainability.' In these terms, therefore, the bailout programme was described as a success, despite its myriad problems: 'Greece remained in the euro area, which was its stated political preference. Spillovers that might have had a severe effect on the global economy were relatively well-contained, aided by multilateral efforts to build firewalls.'[59] Furthermore, despite the probability of Greece being unable to manage her debt pile, 'staff favoured going ahead with exceptional access because of the fear that spillovers from Greece would threaten the euro area and the global economy.'[60] Poul Thomsen, the IMF's lead negotiator in the bailout talks, stated in reference to the signing of the deal in 2010 – despite the lack of any debt relief – that, 'If we were in the same situation … we would have done the same thing again.'[61] Thomsen offered a commitment by European Leaders to do whatever it takes to support Greece, Portugal and Ireland with their bailout-programmes 'even if the headwinds are stronger than expected.'[62] Christine Lagarde commented in a separate interview that, 'What happened at the time, and it's much easier with the benefit of hindsight, is that not all criteria of exceptional access as defined at the time were satisfied' but that 'there was a crying need at the time for support'; however, she also acknowledged that the IMF's experience 'will probably lead us to reassessing the exceptions to the exceptional access criteria', and that it was aiming to make its debt assessments more rigorous.[63] The logic deployed here is therefore that the desperate nature of the situation justified not only the moves made, but any and all mistakes inherent to them. Such questionable reasoning could be used to justify almost any political or financial decision taken in a difficult economic period.

## Greek Fallout in Cyprus

The impact of the bond haircut on the banking system of Cyprus was immediate and catastrophic. PIMCO, in its survey of the financial sector in 2012, estimated that with 'Greek loans represent[ing] about 43 per cent of expected losses on Cyprus and on Greek loans' the aggregate capital shortfall for the participating Cyprus financial institutions would be €6 billion under a 'Baseline' scenario and €8.9 billion under an 'Adverse' scenario. Such assumptions were in fact driven by ironically optimistic projections – notably the 'adverse' scenario highlights a 7.3% loss of GDP in 2012–2015, from peak to trough – far below the over 12% now most likely by the latter year.[64] The report assumed a rise in unemployment to 13.8% in 2013, under the worst-case scenario: instead, it had rocketed to 17.3% by September 2013 (up from the 5% of September 2009), with youth unemployment reaching almost double this number.[65],[66] Yet its outlook still led to the observation that:

> The large banking sector, with assets totalling over 8 times GDP by the broadest measure, and with significant exposure to Greece, is a significant vulnerability. Banks face significant capital needs to reflect mark to market valuations on their sovereign bond holdings and to achieve a 9 per cent core tier one capital ratio, as mandated by the European Banking Authority.[67]

The PIMCO report is indicative of the Troika policy of withholding important information until major aid decisions are made: it appeared on the Internet only after the German Parliament had passed the immediately controversial Cypriot aid package on Thursday, April 18, 2013. Nevertheless, it allows for the collateral damage of the Troika imposed PSI on Greek Government debt to become apparent.

The extent of the banks' exposure to Greek bonds, and its consequence for their balance sheets, was made clear even earlier in the European Banking Authority's 2011 EU-wide 'Stress Tests', published in July as the Troika were hammering out a fresh rescue deal to try and 'save' Greece. The EBA figures showed that 30 per cent, or €11.2 billion, of Bank of Cyprus' total 'credit risk exposure' – defined as EAD, or 'exposure at default' – was tied up in Greece by December 2010, as was 43 per cent (€18.7 billion) of Laiki's (known at the time as 'Marfin Popular Bank').[68] Neither of these banks, however, was included in a bi-annual risk assessment undertaken by the EBA, even as the crisis in Greece unfolded.[69] Bank of Cyprus' 2.4 billion euros of Greek debt was therefore enough to wipe out 75% of the bank's total capital, while Laiki's 3.4 billion euros exposure outstripped its 3.2 billion euros of capital reserves.

Ironically, according to the EBA test, Piraeus Bank had an exposure to Greek sovereign debt weighing in at 271% of its Tier 1 capital – substantially higher than any Cypriot bank.[70] Yet following the decision on October 26, 2011, to write down a large measure of such debt, Piraeus Bank was fully supported, despite its dire capital position. By contrast, Laiki was eventually shut down. As one anonymous source senior to the banking sector described it:

> A political decision was taken to protect the Greek banking system from the instability of the Cypriot banks, so all the damages of the banks were brought to Cyprus. All the losses were born by the Cypriot shareholders of the banks, the Cypriot bondholders and the Cypriot depositors. The Greek banking system was protected, the Cypriot banking system was completely decimated, and this was a political decision: it was not a financial decision taken by the Euro Group of the EU.[71]

Effectively, a decision was taken to impose disproportionate losses on the Cypriot banks. As the European Commission Directorate General Economic and Financial Affairs stated in its Cyprus assessment paper of April 12, 2013: 'The Cypriot banks suffered about €4 billion in losses from the Greek PSI, i.e. more than 22 per cent of GDP...Based on stress tests, including by PIMCO, the capital shortfall of the Cypriot banks is estimated at around €10 billion, after bailing in junior debt holders, or almost 60 per cent of GDP.' As a percentage of GDP, this was the largest bank bailout in history, only narrowly tracking that of Indonesia's by the IMF in 1997.[72]

Christos Triantafyllides, the advocate for Bank of Cyprus shareholders, points out the sudden and calamitous impact of this event:

> ...Its [Cyprus'] banks lost overnight nearly €4.5 billion because the decision was taken in Brussels to haircut the debt of Greece. Cypriot banks were very active in the Greek market. And they were owed a lot of money from the Greek government. When it was decided to haircut the debt of Greece by 50%, overnight Cyprus banks lost €4.5 billion, which brought them very near to collapse.[73]

The scale of the impact of these terms on Cyprus vastly exceeded that of other countries whose banks were notably exposed to Greek debt – and for whose salvation from 'contagion' the various debt deals were at least partly justified. The French toll, by contrast, came to less than 2% of their GDP. Such factors do not appear to have been taken into consideration, and nor did the unique vulnerabilities of the Cypriot banks warrant what even Greek banks received. By contrast, the Hellenic Financial Stability Fund compensated fully any haircut losses of the four systemic Greek banks – Alpha Bank, National Bank of Greece, Eurobank and Piraeus Bank.

Cyprus' banks were effectively Greek banks in disguise. Fifty per cent of the activities of Laiki and Bank of Cyprus were in Greece. As Sarris says, 'Laiki in particular was an independent bank in Greece and it was absorbed by Cyprus about a year earlier. We could have argued that it was not a subsidiary...we could have said we would like these two banks to receive the same treatment as Greek banks which were forced to take the PSI.'[74]

Such considerations were certainly not offered by the Troika. Triantafyllides notes that, 'No protection was given to Cyprus banks, as opposed to protection given to Greek banks...[which] were protected from the haircut that was bound to the debt of the Greek government. This was not done for the Cyprus banks.'

One political source echoes these sentiments:

> Our banking system was tied to the Greek banking system... The same interest rates were applied in Cyprus as they were in Greece, so after 2009 we had very high interest rates: we had all the negative impact from the MoUs without having the support of the MoU in our banking system. Originally the suggestion was to haircut the debt by 20–25% and our banks said OK, we can take that kind of a hit.

The final sum, however, he considers 'disastrous to the Cypriot banks', and translated into 'immediate losses for the banks without any support'. Vassos Shiarly, British Cypriot and AKEL Financial Minister March 2012 to February 2013, suggested on his departure from office that the decision by the Cypriot government to support these measures was an error reflecting the excessive zeal to show solidarity beyond our capabilities to another eurozone country. We should have put some conditions down, and examined how much our pockets could take.[75] Orphanides, in condemnatory language, would later attack what he perceived as 'the communist party's subsequent zeal to exploit the "mistake" for political gain rather than correct it,' and suggest that 'had the government insisted on a more balanced approach to the Greek PSI decision, the banks would not have had problems that could be exploited politically.'[76] In this narrative, AKEL, with the help of the new Central Bank of Cyprus governor Panicos Demetriades, refused their share of the blame by highlighting the collapse of the banking system as the main reason behind the country's current precarious situation. Orphanides argued that to deflect attention from the mismanagement of the economy, 'the communist party assaulted the banks'. He suggests, somewhat cynically, that the label of casino banking promoted by the Central Bank at this time stuck well, and was used effectively against the island and its banking system by proponents of the bail-in.[77]

While a strong case can be made for the government dwelling disproportionately on the banking system to deflect blame in the presidential elections of 2012, it is harder to see how Cyprus, with its limited political clout and historically supportive bond with

Greece, could have dramatically altered the terms offered in the PSI. Triantafyllides notes this problem:

> It would be very, very difficult for any president of Cyprus to oppose a scheme that would save the Greek economy. Bearing in mind the relationship between Cyprus and Greece it would have been very difficult...to stand up and say 'Listen, this decision will destroy my banks, I don't accept it. Because this is saving the economy of Greece.'

In this case, the historic relationship between the Greece and Cyprus – one that had been increasingly fostered to preserve peace and security after 1974 – proved the financial undoing of the latter. The then president of Cyprus could and should have requested the same protection for the Cyprus banks as was afforded to the Greek banks.

It is strikingly clear from the build-up to the banking crisis in Cyprus that the Troika and the ECB *failed to deal in a timely manner* with the fallout from the haircut on Greek sovereign bonds. Effectively, Cyprus was sacrificed on the altar of Greece. As one senior political source anonymously describes this, 'You take a decision to save the economy of one country [when] you know that another country will receive a disproportionate impact to the other European nations, because of the special relationship that it has with Greece; and you do nothing about it.'[78]

At the time, Chancellor Angela Merkel praised the PSI scheme, saying 'We Europeans showed tonight that we reached the right conclusions.' That decision, taken by a combination of European leaders, the IMF and the ECB, set a ticking bomb in the heart of the Cypriot banking system – one that would not only blow a hole right through it within a year, but which also set off a chain reaction of ugly and escalating consequences. A policy of providing massive support for Greece, while kicking the can of Cyprus down the road, turned out to be very costly for all parties concerned.

## Casino Economics and Political Games

When European finance leaders explained their harsh terms for rescuing Cyprus, it proved easy to blame the tiny island's wayward and speculative banking practices for bringing ruin on itself. French Finance Minister Pierre Moscovici offered comments harshly critical of Cyprus in the wake of the final deal, blaming the island's offshore, finance-heavy business model for Cyprus' problems. As he said in a statement to French channel Canal Plus, 'To all those who say we are strangling an entire people ... Cyprus is a casino economy that was on the brink of bankruptcy.' Such sentiments were amplified in the scapegoating remarks of Sigmar Gabriel, the floor leader of the Social Democratic Party (SDP), who blasted the business model of Cyprus for being based on 'Russian oligarchs, Serb mafias, and tax evaders.'[79]

This high moral grandstanding ignores the impact of the EU's deal with Greece on its banking sector. Almost every significant banking institution in Europe took the bonds: it is the *fact* that everyone bought this bad debt that made the Greek deal so important to avoid contagion across the entire financial system. Cyprus differed in the relative *concentration* of the trade – not its financial purpose or first cause.

If 'casino banking' was the sole reason for the existence of such bad trades, this could not explain how French and German banks had roughly a 2% exposure to Greek debt, and Cyprus was over 50%. The historical, economic, cultural and ethnic ties between these two countries, sharpened by their common security interests from 1974, shaped the psychological significance of a massive stake in Greek bonds. This was bolstered both by an eager and sometimes reckless banking culture, and a regulatory infrastructure in the eurozone that actively promoted exactly this type of financial activity. Cypriot banks were effectively Greek banks in the majority of their activities by 2011 – and yet were treated much less favourably by the Troika in the PSI.

The case for the malign influence of this casino banking was made most prominently in the Cypriot establishment by Panicos Demetriades, Governor of the Central Bank of Cyprus from May 2012, as well as ECB Governing Council Member, at a speech for the Hellenic American bankers Association in New York, December 2012, and at the height of the election campaign in Cyprus.[80,81] In his statement, Demetriades recognised that 'public finances have deteriorated rapidly in the last few years', though he points out that 'even after injecting €1.8 billion of public money into one of our banks last June, the country's public debt, currently 83.3% of

GP, remains below that of the euro area average.' The substantial decline that had occurred is not attributed to the escalation in government spending. Instead, 'What has weighed heavily on public finances have been the successive downgrades by ratings agencies, which have long recognised the contingent liability of the large banking sector – imposed on the public finances...' Consequently, 'government finances...have suffered interrelated mounting strains as the difficulties of banks effectively cut off the access of the Cyprus sovereign to international financial markets.'[82] He further suggested that, 'Weakening domestic macroeconomic conditions have also contributed to the deterioration in public finances and the significant consolidation efforts made in the last year or so have not managed to correct the excessive government deficit.'

In January 2012, ten months before this explanation was offered, Standard & Poor's Ratings Services lowered its long-term and short-term sovereign credit ratings on Cyprus by two notches to 'BB+/B' from 'BBB/A-3', with a negative outlook. The agency does indeed cite a financially geared economy as a reason for its bearish forecast, noting 'a relatively concentrated economy' and the 'very high contingent liabilities emanating mostly from its large financial sector.' However, this was far from the only factor held to account: also commented on in the very same paragraph is the country's current account deficit, which averaged 11% of GDP over the course of the AKEL government prior to the report, and a 'politically obstructive environment'.

But above all, the primary cause was seen as exposure to Greek debt and the deteriorating condition of the eurozone. As the agency said:

> The downgrade reflects our view of the systemic stresses – emanating from the eurozone – we see on the large Cypriot financial sector and Cyprus' external asset position, which in our view remains susceptible to a write-down on its high lending exposure to Greece.[83]

Following this, in June 2012 Cyprus' credit rating was cut to junk status by Fitch. The ratings agency explained that the downgrade was mainly due to the exposure of its three largest banks – Bank of Cyprus, Cyprus Popular Bank and Hellenic Bank – to Greek debt.

'Even assuming that Greece remains in the eurozone, Cypriot banks will have to bear significant further loan losses as the Greek economy continues to contract over the medium term as well as the deterioration in domestic asset quality,' it stated.[84] The result of the downgrades to junk status was that government bonds no longer met the eligibility criteria of the ECB. Cyprus became possibly the first nation in modern history whose central bank refused to accept its bonds for the purposes of monetary policy.

It is not hard to argue that these ratings downgrades did not help with either the brewing banking crisis, or the state finances of the island. It is also certainly true that a concentrated financial sector is a factor these agencies cited in their decision. But it is also far from the complete picture. A large financial sector is not the prima facia 'cause' of these debt downgrades: the reports do not cite that as the primary or exclusive factor, and Cyprus was hardly unique in that regard, when compared to Malta, Luxemburg or Great Britain. Rather, it is the relationship between that sector and Greek sovereign debt that wrecked its financial system so comprehensively in early 2012.

Demetriades, in respect to the problem of bank exposure to bonds, argued that the gambling inherent to the 'casino banking culture' on the island manifested in them disproportionately investing too much in the government bond market of a single euro member economy – namely Greece. This, he suggests, violates all the rules and principles of good risk management. As he puts it, 'When one invests over 100% of one's capital in a single financial instrument – even if that instrument is considered low risk – it is indicative of poor risk management... When bankers do the same with investors' money – because their bonuses are linked to short-term income while the losses are underwritten by the taxpayer... it is "casino banking".' It is therefore the failure of the boards of banks to 'exercise proper oversight' that hurt them, and Cyprus, so badly. 'The Greek PSI alone cost Cypriot banks nearly 25% of the country's GDP, because of excessive concentration of Greek debt in the balance sheets of the two largest Cypriot banks.'

Such a precise account of the blame for events in Cyprus by the nation's leading central banker needs to be examined. Without a doubt, a major catalyst of the global financial crisis can be attributed to a collection of practices, innovation and industries that fall under the popular colloquialism of 'casino banking' – most notoriously in the securitisation of US subprime bonds, and the massively leveraged positions in the market attained by US investment banks. There are problems, however, with applying that label quite so easily to the Cypriot situation, and blaming their banks for holding an excess of eurozone bonds. It is hard to pin this exclusively on the greed and recklessness of bankers when the regulatory framework of the EU explicitly encouraged banks to hold government bonds in the same currency, reducing the cost of their financing but creating, as it turned out, a dangerous union that made banks more vulnerable to sovereign risk, and vice versa. Such regulatory encouragement is substantial. The European Union Capital Requirements Directive specifies that the holding of bonds in a country's domestic currency be given a zero-risk weighting against capital.[85] Enshrining these incentives is the zero-risk weighting of such debt by regulators – a decision the Basel Committee on Banking Supervising (BCBC) chose not to reverse in 2010, despite events unfolding in the eurozone.[86]

Under EU rules, therefore, banks can rate all debt issued by the eurozone's governments as risk free, thereby avoiding any increase in their capital requirements. Such preferential treatment made it highly attractive for financial institutions to invest in government bonds. After the onset of the global crisis they became more attractive still, with the rise in the phenomenon of 'carry trading' to exploit the difference in interest rates – with lenders able to borrow at minimal cost from the ECB and plough the money into higher-yielding state debt. The result of this lucrative phenomenon was the share of euro-area sovereign bonds, as a proportion of bank assets, rising from 2008 to 2014 by over 40%, from 4% to 5.7% – the highest relative exposure since 2006.[87]

Of course, just because something is encouraged by the regulatory infrastructure of an institution, does not mean the label has no value. The context in which a financial bubble was fostered is not the full and final explanation for the bubble itself. Yet it is something fundamental to its inception. Much the same observation could be made about the US housing bubble in the 2000s, and the subprime securities derived from it that toxified the financial system: processes which were nurtured both by Alan Greenspan's zero-interest Federal Reserve policy from 2001, and an environment of minimal derivative oversight from 1999.[88] The regulatory infrastructure of the eurozone directly endorsed a concentration in the very kind of debt that was to spell such disaster for the Cypriot banks in the wake of the Greek PSI.

Nikos Papadopoulos suggested in a deposition to the Parliament of Cyprus in 2013 that the problem had not been the existence of a disproportionately large banking system per se, but rather that the increase in national debt from 2008 meant that 'the Government could not safeguard the large deposits that we had in our banking system'. The result was a potential disaster waiting in the wings: 'if the bank ran into trouble there was no safety net to cover its losses', meaning that savings could not be guaranteed by the state.[89] Such a statement is echoed by Sarris, who says 'for consecutive years now we have created excessive public deficits, that have accumulated and reached the point where we can no longer take them', and in the spending warnings offered by various financial institutions in 2009–11.[90] Admittedly, scenarios involving deposits in such extreme jeopardy would have been more or less unthinkable before September 2008. After the collapse of Lehman, however, they became something of a standard practice throughout the developed world; Alistair Darling, the British Chancellor of the Exchequer from 2007–10, described a notorious phone call he received from the chairman of RBS on October 8, 2008, in which he was warned that without a state injection of capital the bank was just several hours away from closing its tills.

Injections of capital, directly or indirectly, and public or covert, became the norm in Cyprus from 2012. The Greek PSI made the banking system of Cyprus dependent on the Emergency Liquidity Assistance (ELA) programme: a device that was essentially a bailout by a eurozone commercial bank by its national central bank, which allows the latter to act as a lender of last resort for stricken, yet supposedly solvent, banks, whose assets do not qualify as collateral for regular ECB financing operations (central banks also charge more for ELA funds as a consequence).

The changing role of such funding reflects the evolution of central banking policy in light of the debt problems of particular eurozone countries, and especially Cyprus. In a widely cited ECB annual report from 1999 that discussed the foundation of the eurozone, the parameters of national central bank assistance were laid down. It suggested this approach to bailing out institutions: 'Central bank support should not be seen as a primary means for ensuring financial stability, since it bears the risk of moral hazard', with 'sound risk management practices' and 'prudential regulation and supervision' seen as the 'first line of defence against excessive risk-taking behaviour and financial distress.

Overseen by the ECB, the terms attached to ELA assistance are therefore highly stringent; that it is deemed 'exceptional', that national central banks have to ensure they receive adequate collateral in exchange, and that they must not engage in 'monetary financing', as in printing money, to prop up their banks. They must also report back to the ECB, which can choose to step in and terminate ELA support with a two-thirds majority vote on its 23-member governing council. At the time, however, it noted that 'the provision of ELA has been a very rare event in industrial countries over the past few decades', presumably rendering such a context and conditions only incidental to the future management of the eurozone.

Such a precedent was rendered irrelevant by the sovereign and banking crises ten years later.[91] Under the rules laid down by the European Central Bank, emergency liquidity assistance loans were only meant to be used by solvent financial institutions. Yet it was this mechanism by which the broken and destitute banks in Ireland and Greece were kept on their feet; and by April 2012, it appears that up to €3.8 billion was held on the balance sheet of the Central Bank of Cyprus in this way.[92] Fifty per cent of the deposits of Laiki were insured in this manner, staving off an otherwise imminent bankruptcy in the wake of the Greek PSI. Such dependence left the island at the throat of its European benefactors. A year later, German Finance Minister Wolfgang Schäuble stated that the Bank of Cyprus and Laiki had become totally dependent on these funds, as the warnings grew from the Troika that they might be cut off if Cyprus did not bow to a bail-in deal.[93]

## From Bailouts to Bail-in

The public consequences of rising deficits, a devastating accident, and the financial damage of the Greek PSI became rapidly apparent even before the deal was finalised and the extent of the haircut was known. From January 2012, Cyprus became reliant on a €2.5bn emergency loan from not the EU but Russia,[94] at an interest rate of 4.5%: economic life-support that allowed the state finances to function by covering an unmanageable budget deficit, and to refinance maturing debt. Although the loan was issued by Russia for 4.5 years, in January 2013 the Cypriots authorities were back asking the Russian government to consider extending it for another five years to 2021. The received loan was expected to cover all refinancing of maturing government debt and the amount needed for the governments continued budget deficits, until the first quarter of 2013 – by January of that year, the government was asking Russia to substantially extend the repayment plan from 2016 to 2021. In January 2012, the government pledged a 1.8 billion euro bailout to Laiki bank – though as Sarris points out, 'they couldn't [pay] even if they wanted to, so they gave them a promissory note which was in essence, junk.' This qualified 'bailout' of Laiki did little to tackle the bond and bad lending debts of the bank, even on top of its assistance from the ELA. The state also recapitalized the CBC in June 2012 with the result that the government acquired 84% of the bank's equity. This increased the bank's core tier 1 capital ratio to 9%, as now mandated by the European Banking Authority.

With Russia holding a substantial portion of the over €20 billion in non-eurozone bank accounts, it is little surprise that they had been ready and willing to help Nicosia stave off the day of reckoning. But the Russian loan did not include any funds for recapitalization of the Cypriot financial sector; indeed, it was generally expected Cyprus would need to apply for an additional bailout loan.[95] It could not fix the sustainability problems of either the government's budget or broken banking sector. Indeed it may have visibly worsened their perception. As Sarris put it, 'the reply [to the crisis] was instead of taking measures to address the irregularities in your economy you seek money from your friends the Russians, then it shows there are deep irregularities in your system ... [and] problems regarding the stability of our banking sector'.[96] The loan did, however, postpone its resolution to a later date – conveniently enough, after the next presidential election in February 2013.

This does not mean that steps were not taken to contain the mounting budgetary problems of the state. They do, however, appear to have been hobbled by the ideological parameters of an AKEL

administration. The government proposed a four-year, €1bn adjustment programme to turn the economy around, starting with a
fourth-quarter rise in tax revenues of €100m, equal to about 0.7 per
cent of national output. The EU and IMF had called for savings of
€975m between 2012 and 2015, with €175m of cuts to be made by
December: savings predicated on cutting the salaries paid to about
70,000 civil servants who make up the largest sector of the island's
workforce. As it was, the government showed no desire to implement such measures, or reduce the pensions and privileges upon
which its term in power from 2008 had been consciously defined.
Theodore Panayotou, director of the Cyprus Institute for International Management, called the measures offered 'a simple accounting
exercise... that totally misses the point. Even though taxes will be
higher, the expected revenue increases will not materialise.'[97]

In the face of international pressure, the now almost insolvent government of President Demetris Christofias declared in June of 2012
that it sought an EU bailout – becoming the fifth eurozone country to
do so – just days before a deadline to recapitalise one of the country's
largest banks: 'The purpose of the required assistance is to contain the
risks to the Cypriot economy, notably those arising from the negative
spillover effects through its financial sector, due to its large exposure
in the Greek economy,' the government said in a statement offered
on June 25.[98]

But if European leaders had hoped Cyprus meant its public call
for aid to signal a westward break from its Moscow benefactors, the
country's (Soviet-educated) president made clear they would be dis-
appointed. A week after declaring it desired assistance from Brussels,
Demetris Christofias said his government sought a further rescue loan
of €5 billion from the Kremlin; implicitly using the threat of borrowing from Russia as a way to force the EU to exact less onerous
terms. As it happened, further assistance from the Kremlin did not
materialise, and the attempt to bargain off Russia against the EU may
have had the opposite effect than was desired in the terms of March
2013. As Sarris puts it, 'The average time the other countries of the
EU sought assistance from the application... was weeks, for Ireland,
Portugal, Spain. In our case we started applying in June 2012, and we
had a conclusion in March 2013... the delay may be because of the
[Cypriot Presidential] elections and the previous government didn't

want the political cost of taking assistance.' He suggests this produced a 'much harsher support programme' that 'led to the complete collapse of the banking system.'[99] While these explanations are ultimately conjecture, they fit the facts of what happened – namely, that the desired assistance was not forthcoming, no deal was arranged, and the country remained on financial life support for the remainder of the presidential term.

# 4
# Bailouts and Bail-Ins

## The Cyprus Experiment

In the previous chapter, we have examined both the immediate and underlying causes of the crisis. Here we are looking at the final stages of the crisis itself, culminating in the 'bail-in' rescue package of March/April 2013. This new and previously untested approach was, it will be argued, the EU-IMF's latest weapon in its austerity armoury for dealing with financially wayward members of the eurozone.

Road-testing this technique on Cyprus has an obvious logic to it. The economy of the island was too small for anything more than a ripple effect for this new modus operandi, at least in direct financial terms: minimising the systemic consequences which the entire approach was crafted to avoid.[1] The country's plutocratic ties outside the eurozone made the policy much easier to sell to the European media, if not to the people of Cyprus themselves. The bail-in served the purpose of avoiding the use of taxpayers' money to bail *out* the very banks that had contributed to the problem in the first place: the central, and enormously unpopular, characteristic of bank rescue plans since the collapse of Lehman Brothers in 2008.

The plans for dealing with this new approach were encouraged by the belief, as it was promoted to the EU parliament and the press, that this time it would be the bank *depositors* – many of them Russian, and apparently therefore rich, unscrupulous profiteers – who would fund a substantial part of the rescue package, thereby sparing the taxpayer from direct involvement. This is despite the fact that taxpayers would inevitably be directly or indirectly affected by the very measures (entrenched in the MoU) of the rescue programme devised to resolve the crisis. Many if not most of these depositors were Cypriot residents and EU nationals with modest investments, seeking out returns not available in other eurozone banks where deposit rates were at an all-time low of 1–2%. Under this scheme, small business owners and holders of private pension schemes and retirement savings would be just as likely to take a hit as the very wealthy, and were substantially more numerous as clients.

Throughout the winter of 2012–13, high-level discussions took place between the institutions of the Troika and a group of EU member states, led by Germany, on how to absorb the financing needs of Cyprus. With the ballooning banking crisis and the steady deterioration in the public purse, these now amounted to almost €17 billion: of which around €10 billion were needed to recapitalise the banks, and the rest to cover the fiscal shortfall at a state level.

These two strong external constraints reduced much of the potential room for manoeuvre: the fact that the IMF insisted strongly on a debt-to-GDP ratio of not more than 100% by 2020 far stricter than imposed on Greece; and the fact that key eurozone member states, including Germany, made clear that programme financing should not exceed €10 billion. The approach was not only uncompromisingly tough: it ignored the fact that it was Cyprus that was the most hardest hit when its banks (Laiki and Bank of Cyprus) lost 50% of their capital in the Greek PSI deal.

Formal application for EU assistance was delayed until June 2012. It should have been made much earlier in the light of the damage wrought by the Greek PSI, when €4.8 billion was wiped off the balance sheets of Laiki and the Bank of Cyprus. Whatever motivations can be firmly ascribed to this, it was certainly in the political interests of the previous AKEL government to postpone any tough, Troika-mandated resolution until after the presidential elections of 2013, to avoid the fallout from such assistance.

Cypriot politicians quickly came to realise that any rescue would involve a quid pro quo in itself. As one source in the government commented:

> It is interesting to note that from the beginning, opinion was talking about a problem for Cyprus that would reach about 17 billion euros. By December 2012 it was decided that they would give no

money to the banks; they would give 10 billion for government financing needs.

Effectively a statement was made that 'you are going to have to find the money for the banks yourselves. That meant a decision was taken that a deposit would be haircutted.'[2] This view also finds credence in statements made by many politicians to the programme agreement: not least Chancellor Merkel, who with her mind on her own German forthcoming elections, stated flatly... 'the banks must take responsibility for themselves. That's what we have always said. We don't want taxpayers having to save banks but that banks must save themselves.'[3] Merkel was in no mood to alienate a German electorate already critical of the existing bailouts of its southern neighbours. As a former banking supervisor put it, 'bailing out Russian oligarchs with European Stability Mechanism taxpayer money would not be possible in a German election year.'[4] Added to this, 'A secret German intelligence report conducted in Cyprus' suggested that substantial beneficiaries of the package 'would be rich Russians who had invested illegal money there,' the German weekly *Der Spiegel* wrote in November, 2012. 'It's a big dilemma for Chancellor Angela Merkel.'[5] It must be noted, however, that the report focused on the Russian and Ukrainian depositors of the two main banks, Laiki and Bank of Cyprus, but ignored the fact that both banks had many Cypriot and other EU (and non-EU depositors) on their books. *Der Spiegel* drew the rather bizarre conclusion from this that '... the beneficiaries of the help won't be ordinary workers or farmers but a caste of nouveauriche immigrants that shamelessly boast their wealth while making virtually no contribution to solving the country's problems.' As if the banking crisis and its resolution was irrelevant to the ordinary citizens of the island – and as if people without extreme wealth had no substantial savings of their own.

From early March until the final agreement was hammered out at the eleventh hour in Brussels (on March 25, 2013) the new government was in constant and intense negotiations with the Troika. The plan that was being tabled to rescue Cyprus was unprecedented in its nature. In the case of previous eurozone debt crises – notably those of Greece, Ireland, and Portugal – only bail-*out* provisions were applied to the rescue package and austerity programme, however brutal and divisive the latter tenets came to be. But the direct implications of the bailout were, by their very nature, contained to taxpayers, rather than depositors. To safeguard the banking system, savings were treated as sacred. Every financial or sovereign debt bailout since the beginning of the financial crisis had operated on this principle, whatever the consequences or cost.

But Cyprus gave the Troika the opportunity to try something different. Its wider significance was immediately flagged on March 25, when Eurogroup President Jeroen Dijsselbloem said that Cyprus could serve as a template for future EU bailouts. Although he was quick to rescind the statement, the retraction does not exactly restore confidence this was not on their minds.[6]

Under the moralising banner of 'casino banking', and protestations about the financial influence of Russian oligarchs, the Eurogroup could insist that depositors contribute to recapitalising the broken banks, and binding them in to the rescue package. In the words of one top former banking executive, 'the bloated Cyprus offshore banking centre offers a "gift from heaven" that European finance ministers cannot refuse.'[7] In this climate, there was little appetite for any of the more moderate suggestions put forward by the Cypriot side. Michael Sarris, Finance Minister at the time, described his experience of the negotiations: 'We said we were confident we could give a satisfactory plan that would make the debt sustainable, we will raise taxes and cut expenditure, we would put taxes on interest rates ... [They] went on to say that they were not keen to follow through on this approach because of previous experience.'[8]

The option favoured by Germany and the IMF was for a *significant* bail-in of uninsured depositors in Cyprus' two biggest banks, Bank of Cyprus and Laiki. But the EU Commission had serious reservations about this and took a more considered view, both due to the impact it was feared it would have on financial stability – since it could easily be seen as a precedent – and because of the impact on the Cypriot economy, as many Cypriot businesses would face substantial capital losses.

In his statement to the European Parliament on the April 17, 2013, Olli Rehn, Vice-President of the European Commission, and member responsible for Economic and Monetary Affairs and the euro, emphasised that 'the Commission's preferred scenario was a more gradual adjustment of the Cypriot banking system and real economy, while ensuring debt sustainability.' He also acknowledged in his address that even though the formal request for financial assistance had not been made by the Cyprus government until June 2012, 'After a half year of talks, a staff-level agreement on the necessary structural reforms and fiscal measures was reached. Many of them, including anti-money laundering measures, were adopted by the Cypriot parliament before the end of 2012.'⁹ Rehn also explained the financial constraints operating on the Commission: only €10 billion of support had been pledged to a bailout, 'whereas the total financing needs had been estimated at €17 billion euros.' Consequently, 'This constraint severely limited the options available.'

The most significant of these initial options was the idea of a general levy on all bank deposits, which dwarfed all other suggestions. Sources familiar with the discussions that took place at the time suggested the Commission's view was that if a levy on deposits were introduced, it should be kept at a low level of the total capital: for instance 2 or 3%, and certainly not higher than 5%. A levy of around 3% would have been roughly equivalent to a 100% withholding tax on one year's interest income; since Cypriot banks have been paying account holders around that level of interest, or even higher, which is far in excess of the mean rate in the eurozone.

According to sources familiar with these discussions, the EU Commission had serious reservations with this approach, concerned as they were with the impact it would have both on financial stability, and the losses for Cypriot commercial businesses. Capital controls would inevitably have to be applied to avoid a Depression-era style bank run. The measure could also send alarmist signals to other eurozone states in debt difficulty (for example Italy and Spain) that deposits were no longer considered inviolate by the Troika. The risk, then, was of such a remedy causing the kind of financial contagion it sought to contain.

However, during the Eurogroup's discussion on the night of March 15/16, Germany and the IMF made clear that if the levy option were to be decided upon, rather than a full bail-in, it would need to be applied much more broadly. The plan had to raise at least €5.8bn, and no other fiscal measures being floated offered the certainty or swift capacity to generate immediate revenue.

A number of other options were explored as alternatives, without success. A flat levy of 5% across the board, and a variable one of 3%, 5% and 7% for different levels of deposits, was unequivocally rejected by the European Commission. The Cyprus representatives attempted to commit to covering the financing gap of €5.8 billion by introducing a levy of 6.75% and 9.9% on deposits. This plan, however, quickly unravelled in the following days. Finally, the Eurogroup put forward a proposal for a levy of 5% and 12.5% for deposits above and below €100,000, receiving the backing of the IMF and the Commission: this was rejected by President Anastasiades, who made clear he would not accept a levy over 10% for uninsured depositors (those over €100,000).

At this point the Cypriot delegation – during the Eurogroup conference call of March 18 – *did not move to amend the structure of the levy to exempt insured depositors entirely*: although by this point this was the view of the rest of the Eurogroup (all ministers and the three Troika representatives). The Cypriot representative made clear that the high levy this would have implied on uninsured deposits would not be acceptable. As a result of this impasse, Jörg Asmussen, a German economist representing the executive branch of the ECB, confirmed to the Cypriots that ELA funding would be shut off for Laiki Bank the following week (from March 25, 2013) in the absence of an agreement on a rescue programme.

The emergency liquidity loans programme had been a noose around the neck of the banking system since the beginning of 2012: now it was being tightened. The effect of this withdrawal would be drastic. It would almost certainly have led to the collapse of Laiki, leading to either its liquidation under existing Cypriot insolvency law, since no bank resolution framework was yet in place, or simply to a disorderly bankruptcy. A liquidation under such circumstances would have to treat all creditors according to the insolvency laws; therefore allowing for no distinction between depositors, bondholders and shareholders. Since the government would have to compensate all 'insured' depositors from the public purse with money it did not have, this would in turn have pushed the Cypriot state towards an immediately default, and possible even an exit from the euro.

With the rejection of all posited versions of the levy by the Cypriot House of Representatives on March 19, the mounting financial pressures on Laiki, coupled with the expected withdrawal of ELA money, made it a priority for the Cyprus Parliament to adopt the procedure of bank resolution and inevitable capital restrictions, followed by a programme to be agreed to avoid the looming sovereign default.

Yet the meeting of the Eurogroup on March 25 made it clear that there were no new ideas or solutions to be discussed, and a painful decision had to be made. Finding the least painful solution remained the overriding problem for the new government and what Parliament would assent to in the end. One senior political source, who wishes to remain anonymous, took the view that the President was effectively strong-armed in this decision:

> ...there is a new President there, who came in only seven days before. He goes there, he asks for time, to see if he can find some solution, other than this extremely brutal one, and you don't give it him. And you tell him that it's Friday and if you don't accept, your banks do not open on Monday. Which means, effectively, that you bring down the banking system and take the country to bankruptcy.[10]

What was finally agreed was neither the preferred option of the EU Commission, nor a popular outcome for the Cypriot people, saddled as they were with an unprecedented panacea for the economic problems incurred on the island.

On March 25 the arrangements with the Cyprus government centred on the closure of Laiki bank and a plan for the recapitalisation for Bank of Cyprus (BOC). The deposits below 100K, together with the remaining healthy assets, were annexed and transferred to the Bank of Cyprus.[11] Laiki was split into a 'good' and 'bad' bank – the good bank emerged with Bank of Cyprus and the entered a process of being unwound. The board and CEO of Laiki were replaced on March 27.

The recapitalisation of the Bank of Cyprus was conducted in the following manner:

1. Uninsured depositors (over 100K) received 'A' shares worth €1 with full voting and dividend rights. This applied to 37.5% of the uninsured deposits. Senior debt was converted into 'B' shares, with subordinated debt into 'C' shares, convertible capital instruments into 'D' shares (capital instruments that act as bonds but convert to equity in given circumstances) with the rights of ordinary shareholders being suspended with *no dividends or voting rights* until the 'A' shares regained their capital investment with interest.

2. This structure implied a preliminary 37.5% conversion ratio on uninsured deposits and of the remaining 62.5%, a further 22.5% was to remain frozen until an independent audit of the bank assets and liabilities was conducted, as required by the bank resolution framework by the end of June 2013. The final 40% could be withdrawn by depositors in stages with the final stage set for September 2014.
3. The Greek branches of the Bank of Cyprus were sold off on March 26 as part of the overall agreement to Piraeus Bank in Greece (as discussed below).
4. As a result of these resolution measures, the Bank of Cyprus has essentially absorbed the largest part of the operations of Laiki Bank in Cyprus and continues to provide services to the customers of both banks, through the branches of the Bank of Cyprus and the branches of the former Laiki Bank.

A substantial reform of the financial sector had been at the corner-stone of the deal, and was enshrined in the EU's subsequent Memorandum of Understanding.[12] Under the terms of this agreement of March 25, the Cyprus Parliament adopted the necessary framework legislation to establish the Central Bank of Cyprus as the single authority for all the banks and co-operative credit institutions.[13] The resolution measures for Laiki included the sale of its branches in Greece to Piraeus bank and the sale of its business in Cyprus to the Bank of Cyprus. All relevant contracts and obligations were also transferred to either the Bank of Cyprus or Piraeus Bank. The 'insured' deposits in Laiki were also transferred to BOC for both individuals and legal entities. The entire savings of other financial institutions including the government, municipalities local councils insurances companies, charities, educational establishments and deposits belonging to JCC payment systems (the primary processor of card transactions in Cyprus) were also transferred. All other 'uninsured' deposits above €100K remained in the Laiki 'bad bank'. All loans and credit facilities to Laiki clients were transferred to the Bank of Cyprus. The Eurogroup, in the Annex to its Statement made on March 25, said that Laiki would be resolved with the full contribution of equity shareholders, bond holders and uninsured depositors, based on a decision by the central Bank of Cyprus, using the newly adopted Bank Resolution Framework. They also specified that Laiki would be split into a 'good bank' and a 'bad bank'. The bad bank would be run down over time.[14]

The overall effect of these measures was to reduce the size of the domestic banking sector as a proportion of GDP from over 550% to 350%. The Bank of Cyprus would be fully recapitalised and be eligible to participate in the ongoing monetary policy operations of the eurozone.

On the April 30, 2013, the Cypriot Parliament formerly gave its approval to the terms already agreed, endorsing the rescue package which was outlined in the Troika's MoU agreement (version April 12, 2013) and which included the following provisions: the recapitalisation of the entire financial sector while accepting the closure of Laiki bank; fiscal consolidation to help bring down the Cypriot state budget deficit; structural reforms to restore competitiveness macroeconomic imbalances; and extensive privatisation programmes of major industries.

The final conditions incorporated the 'implementation of the anti-money laundering framework in Cypriot financial institutions'.[15] A fairly positive assessment in this regard had been undertaken earlier in 2011 by MONEYVAL,[16] but now as part of the conditions for the bailout, fresh audits were conducted by both Deloitte Financial Advisory and MONEYVAL in April 2013 to check that a robust regime was in place to implement anti-money laundering measures (AML). These audits were among the most rigorous to be conducted in the EU and demonstrated how stringent AML implementation would be applied to bailout (or bail-in) applicants in the future. There was concern expressed by the CBC that the Troika summary of the two AML reports failed to highlight the main positive findings.... 'but rather a description of the perceived weaknesses of the system, drawing inferences where none exist in the original reports.'[17]

The ramifications of the decisions taken in the rescue package that affected both individuals and legal and non-entities were, and continue to be, far reaching. They remain the subject of ongoing litigation in the Cypriot courts. Those legal entities which were covered in the list of exemptions from the haircut/levy proved a major bone of contention with depositors of Laiki and the Bank of Cyprus – arguing as they did that they bore the full burden of the savings haircut at the expense of others. The argument was raised that the resolution measures placed depositors in a worse position than if Laiki bank had been wound up under normal company law procedures. On this point, Triantafyllides, as Advocate for the Bank of Cyprus shareholders, makes this case for the defence:

> Banks are private companies and as a shareholder you have invested in that private company and since that private company faced financial difficulties the value of your shares diminished along with the value of the entity in which you invested. If the Bank of Cyprus was valued in accordance with internationally accepted valuation principles... [18]

The depositors' legal basis for claiming was against the two banks for default in not paying according their contractual obligations. They would issue proceedings for a breach of contract law against the Bank of Cyprus and Laiki in a civil action for damages in the District Courts of the Republic, reserving of potential claims against the CBC as the legal supervisory body; and potentially government departments if previous statements made by state officials as to the creditworthiness of the bank are proven.

The civil proceedings would allow the courts to examine whether the banks had breached their contractual obligations towards claimants as a result of state and/or European intervention, and whether this intervention violates the Constitution of the Republic of Cyprus and European law.[19] In order to be successful in any claims against the Banks and/or the state, claimants will need to prove that the resolution or rescue of the credit institution concerned has put them in a worse financial position than they would have been in, had the credit institution been liquidated under Article 3(2)(d) of the Resolution of Credit and other Institutions Law of 2013 (Law 17(I)/2013).

An initial Supreme Court of Cyprus judgement was made in respect of the first 53 cases filed by depositors against the bail-in levy, when the Central Bank of Cyprus (CBC) exercised its decree directly affecting loss of their property rights. The Attorney General had already fended off a class action on the basis that the CBC was immune from actions in this case. The Supreme Court subsequently decided on July 7, 2013 that the depositors had no *locus standi* – or formal legal grounds – to pursue their actions there. The court didn't examine the merits or consequences of levy in its own right, as it was deemed not an issue of a *public nature*. However, it did recognise the right of depositors to claim damages for their losses in the civil courts, and guided them to follow this route through civil actions in the Cyprus District Courts. This was without them having to dispute the administrative actions that caused them the loss in the first place.[20]

The Supreme Court also clarified an essential issue with respect to their ruling out of the objections of the CBC and the Republic of Cyprus. This was that the defence of 'Acts of Government'[21] could not be used by them in any breach of contract case to be pursued by depositors against Laiki or Bank of Cyprus. On the principle of *'The state is not above the law'*, the Supreme Court affirmed that the CBC could not claim legal immunity for its actions to escape liability where, at least, the depositors could prove that they would have been better off but for the specific decrees of the central bank. The Court also added that the depositors may pursue action against the state for having caused the breach of the contractual obligation in the exercise of the Decree. The list of defendants could extend to those government departments to include the CBC or even the Ministry of Finance, to the extent that the actions of the state/Republic and its organs caused harm to the depositors, by putting them in a worse position than they would have been if the decrees had not been issued. There may also be a case for adding EU institutions as co-defendants.

With final parliamentary approval on April 30, the Troika worked with the Cyprus authorities to support them with the orderly resolution of Laiki and restructuring of Bank of Cyprus, and to finalise the MoU so that the programme could be implemented without any further delay. The final agreement stuck closely to that consistently pursued by the IMF and endorsed by its Managing Director Christine Lagarde, who on March 24 made this statement on the freshly finalised agreement:

> The agreement reached today on Cyprus provides a comprehensive and credible plan to deal with the current economic challenges in the country. The plan focuses on dealing with the two problem banks and fully protecting insured deposits in all banks.... This agreement provides the basis for restoring trust in the banking system, which is key to supporting growth. We believe the plan provides a durable and fully financed solution to the

underlying problems facing Cyprus and places it on a sustainable path to recovery.[22]

That this would measure easily seen as an 'experiment' for the eurozone, and not simply the punishment of a singularly and uniquely wayward island state – the image the Troika was so keen to seize on and promote – was inevitable. Revealing statements by EU leaders on the subject aside, the opportunity was just too perfect. As Triantafyllides puts it,

> I have no doubt that they used Cyprus as a guinea pig to test the principle, because the size of the Cyprus economy is such that they run no risk if something goes wrong. They couldn't do it for example with Italy or Spain . . . . yet there is no domino effect. If they did this with a huge economy and it went wrong, it would overflow into the economies of other countries. The Cyprus economy is too small to have a domino effect. [23]

## International Reactions to the Bail-In

Responses from the European Parliament were numerous and frequently condemnatory, especially from the back benches. Nessa Childers, the MEP for Ireland East was one of a number of MEPs who were vocal in expressing their disquiet to the Cyprus Bailout terms. In a letter dated March 19, 2013, she made her feelings clear:

> Today I have written to the European Commission President Barroso requesting that he ask for the resignation of Commissioner Rehn over the Cypriot bailout fiasco.[24]

She went on to claim that

> The Troika deal, which Commissioner Rehn was centrally responsible for, to impose losses on small Cypriot depositors with less than EUR 100,000 was a terrible mistake and that such harsh measures are simply unfair, undemocratic . . . the decision to impose losses on small depositors and family savers has crossed an extremely important red line in the crisis. The decision must be reversed immediately.

She further argued that the Cyprus bailout

> strengthens the case for more accountability and transparency around Troika decisions. The European Parliament should have a veto over the appointment of Troika chiefs, with regular report-backs to the relevant parliament committee and the right to audit Troika actions. Parliament should ensure that Troikas respect core EU principles, including social justice and social cohesion.

Such a viewpoint was hardly uncommon. Sharon Bowles, the chair-woman of the European Parliament's Economic and Monetary Affairs Committee and MEP for South East England, said she was appalled by the plans for a levy. 'This grabbing of ordinary depositors' money is billed as a tax, so as to try and circumvent the EU's deposit guarantee laws. It robs smaller investors of the protection they were promised.'[25] Guy Verhofstadt, a Belgian MEP and leader of the ALDE liberal group referred to the handling of the Cyprus Crisis as 'a disaster. It gives the impression that Europe is failing – what's failing is the bad inter-governmental system we have today.' Hannes Swoboda, the Austrian Centre-Left MEP, claimed that the Troika had been unacceptably dis-missive of Cypriot ministers. Mr Swoboda told Olli Rehn: 'You are responsible to this Parliament, the Troika is not', and attacked what he described as 'how they treated the elected President of Cyprus and their rude behaviour to the elected representatives of Cyprus' and as 'not acceptable'.[26]

Such views were echoed throughout the media at large. In its Schumpeter blog, *The Economist*, a publication which had not expressed particular sympathy to the political and financial deci-sions of Greek Cypriots since the rejection of the Annan Plan, called The Cyprus haircut arrangement: 'Unfair, short-sighted and self-defeating', writing:

> The Cypriot deal has no coherence in the larger context. The Euro Crisis has been in abeyance for a few months, thanks largely to the readiness of the European Central Bank to intervene to help struggling countries. The ECB's price for helping countries is to insist they go into a bail-out programme. The political price of going into a programme has just gone up, so the ECB's safety net looks a little thinner.

The bail-out appears to move Europe further away from the institutional reforms that are needed to resolve the crisis once and for all. Rather than using the European Stability Mechanism to recapitalise banks, and thereby weaken the link between banks and their governments, the euro zone continues to equate bank bail-outs with sovereign bail-outs. As for debt mutualisation, after imposing losses on local depositors, the price of support from the rest of Europe is arguably costlier now than it ever has been.[27]

Economist Richard D. Wolff commented in an interview in relation to the Cyprus bailout agreement as follows:

This is blackmail. This is basically the officials of the banks and the political leaders going to the mass of people and saying to them, 'This awful deal that makes you, who have nothing to do with the crisis and didn't get any bailout, pay the costs of the crisis and the bailout. You must do this, because if you don't, we will do even more damage to you and your economy. So give us your deposits, give us your money, pay more taxes, suffer fewer social programs, because if you don't, we will impose even worse on you.' It's the basic idea of austerity across the board and in our country, too. And I think it's the confrontation of a system that does not work with the mass of the people, saying, 'We will go down and take you with us, unless you bail us out'.[28]

It is no surprise that the Russian response was less than favourable, and Premier Dmitry Medvedev added a strong voice to the chorus of discontent. 'All possible mistakes that could be made have been made by them,' he said. 'The measure that was proposed is of a confiscation nature, and unprecedented in its character. I can't compare it with anything but ... decisions made by Soviet authorities ... when they didn't think much about the savings of their population.' He further argued that as 'we are living in the 21st century, under market economic conditions', this meant that 'ownership rights should be respected.'[29]

In Britain, Alistair Darling, Chancellor of the Exchequer for the Labour government from 2007–10, criticised the bail-in/levy plan when he stated:

... they have actually now said to people 'We will come after your deposits, no matter how small your savings are' and that seems to me to make it more likely that, if you are a saver in Spain or Italy, for example, and you have just a sniff of the EU or the IMF coming your way, you will take your money out and you will get a run on the bank. So what they are doing is everything you shouldn't do when you are trying to solve a problem like this.

Darling, echoing the widely touted notion of casino banking, said he felt little sympathy with anybody 'who happens to be parking their money in a Cypriot bank' and that 'the way to sort that out is to grab hold of these banks, to do the restructuring you need and to tighten up the controls that are singularly lacking in some of these countries.'[30]

Also critical of the mechanism of the bail-in was British Chancellor George Osborne, who told the Treasury Committee that plans to impose a levy on bank deposits were a 'mistake' and had 'not been well handled'. He went on to say: '... but you have to respect the fact that it's a newly elected president facing incredibly difficult decisions,' explaining to MPs that the Cypriot President Nicos Anastasiades had only been in the job for a matter of weeks before the bailout was negotiated.[31]

The Chancellor was also keen to suggest that the UK had not been kept privy or been given prior knowledge of the original plan to impose a broader bank levy, which would have involved small depositors (below €100K) effectively being charged 6.75% of their deposits to fund the bailout. 'Had the measure been imposed,' he said, 'very considerable damage would have been done to the principle of deposit insurance.' Whether such damage was substantially avoided by the terms that *were* imposed is of course a separate matter to consider.

The substantial military and expatriate British presence on this former colony gave the Chancellor plenty of incentive to speak up about the crisis. Osborne was quick to reassure the 3000 servicemen based in the Sovereign Base Areas (SBAs) at Akrotiri and Dhekelia in Cyprus that they would not be affected by the banking levy, announcing on March 17 that the government had flown out to Cyprus an extra €13m in cash to provide funds for military personnel and civil service staff working in the SBAs. Indeed he offered this statement of support on *The Andrew Marr Show*:

> For people serving in our military, for people serving our Government out in Cyprus – because we have military bases there – we are going to compensate anyone who is affected by this bank tax. People who are doing their duty for our country in Cyprus will be protected from this Cypriot bank tax.[32]

But no such protection was offered to the 59,000 UK expatriates on the island, with some estimates putting the cost of the levy at €170 million. The Bank of Cyprus UK assured its customers in Britain that their deposits would not be affected by the levy, as it is a UK bank separately incorporated in the UK (as a subsidiary) and so depositors were protected by UK Financial Services Compensation Scheme (FSCS). As it stated on its website to customers: 'Bank of Cyprus UK Ltd is a separately capitalised UK incorporated bank, is subject to UK financial regulation and eligible depositors are protected by the UK's Financial Services Compensation Scheme.' Laiki Bank UK, although not a formal subsidiary and with only a small branch network in the UK, was also able to assure its British customers their deposits would not be affected. Technically, the UK operations of Laiki were directly controlled from Cyprus, and so were *not* covered under the UK FSCS. But under the Cyprus Deposit Protection Fund,[33] Laiki UK's 15,000 accounts, totalling 270 million in value, were moved to the UK subsidiary of Bank of Cyprus to escape the haircuts imposed upon its customers in Cyprus.[34]

In response to a growing tide of criticism about the manner in which the Troika tackled Cyprus, a statement was made in the European Parliament by Ollie Rehn on April 17, 2013, at the European Commission. In his statement he offered a background narrative to justify the extraordinary nature of the bail-in:

> The problems of Cyprus built up over many years. At their heart was an oversized banking sector that thrived on attracting foreign deposits with very favourable conditions. These capital inflows also contributed to a property boom and the accumulation of external imbalances.

Rehn went on to blame the Cypriot banks for 'poor risk management' and the fact they 'were allowed to build up by far too concentrated risk exposures'. He thereby pinned the entire sovereign and economic problems of the state and country on the faults of the banking sector – the justification *par excellence* in this crisis.[35]

The fact that Cyprus only officially began to ask for financial assistance in June 2012 (although the signing of the MoU was delayed for nearly a year) put pressure on the decision-making process. Rehn went on further to say 'the Commission's preferred scenario was a more gradual adjustment of the Cypriot banking system and real economy, while ensuring debt sustainability.' By the time the bailout deal was being negotiated, Rehn informed the European Parliament that, 'The scenario of a more gradual economic adjustment was not on the cards anymore, unfortunately.'[36] These statements did not give any explanation for why the euro member states were prepared only to commit up to €10 billion when the total financial needs were estimated at €17 billion.

The consequence for Cypriots of both the bail-in and its associated austerity measures were manifold. EU economists, together with their IMF counterparts, forecast that the Cyprus economy would contract by a devastating 8.7% in 2013 (and a further 3.9% in 2014) – a number surpassing Greece in the throes of her austerity depression. They said that 17% of the Cypriot workforce would be out of a job this year – up from an original projection of 15.5% – while unemployment would hit 19.6% in 2014, not 16.9%.[37]

The immediate impact of the levy went far beyond the loss of 'uninsured' deposits by savers. Unsurprisingly, it profoundly eroded the trust of both foreign and domestic depositors. Confidence in Cyprus' banks took a nose dive as a consequence of the bail-in of depositors, leading to a continued flight of deposits despite the government's imposition of capital controls to stem the outflow.[38] As Michalis Antoniou (the Assistant Director General of the Cyprus Employers & Industrialists Federation OEB) explains:

There was no distinction between savings and working capital above the insured thresholds. So the knock-on effect from getting no access to any form of liquidity, any capital, any payment of wages, means that the employees cannot get paid, so they cannot go to the supermarkets to buy food [until normal banking business was restored].[39]

The exchange controls on capital movement had a severe impact on the whole banking system. It was an essential feature of the resolution to avoid capital outflows from the island, but the measure was nonetheless a natural consequence of the draconian conditions implemented, which do not appear to have been thought through sufficiently at the time.

The practical, day-to-day implications of the bail-in eroded confidence in the whole Cyprus banking system; for local and foreign depositors, commercial and individual clients. It is hard to estimate how many were able to pull out of from their exposed positions before it was too late. Chris Hadjisoteriou, a retired businessman and investor who had made a number of substantial deposits in the banks: 'I was fortunate in taking action with my personal finances just before in January 2013 in fact.' Such fortuitous fears were stimulated by reading the international press as much as local Cypriot newspapers. As he says, 'For some reason I became concerned and decide to redeem the bond deposited with Laiki bank who initially refused only offering to do so if I generated additional business with them.' For him the matter was resolved satisfactorily; others were less fortunate, and more than a few were left infuriated by the varied fortunes of different clients of the banks. 'People are very, very angry especially as they know that some people, mysteriously, got their money out before the bank doors slammed.'[40]

Little of the €10 billion bail-out was reserved for the recapitalisation of the banks – save for €1.5 billion put aside to recapitalise the smaller Cooperative banks in Cyprus, due to the social and ethical premise under which they operated. The package was earmarked to deal with the public sector deficit – but covering its costs is a different matter to dealing with its institutional problems. As Antoniou argues:

> When we talk about the public sector debt this is to pay for all the salaries of a bloated public sector. This includes the police forces as well as the teachers, the army and the whole of the civil service which amounts to 72,000 people.

The Federation of Employers and Industrialists had for some time been advocating prudence in the public finances:

We have been asking, I mean the Employers Federation . . . to limit the pace with which we increase public expenditure, if we would have done that then no troubles would have happened because we would have been able to safeguard the banking sector and avoid the international intervention in our internal affairs.[41]

Pivotal to the rescue plan was a comprehensive restructuring of the banking sector. This included the smaller cooperative banks, where some closures and mergers would be undertaken with the support of the €1.5 billion euros earmarked in the rescue package. This would subsequently be used to recapitalise them. 'The largest challenge for the banks is to deal with deteriorating asset quality. The key here will be to develop plans to ensure that all banks achieve a return of confidence and a return to profitability,' said Delia Velculescu, IMF Mission Chief for Cyprus. This theme was taken up in a speech she gave in Nicosia on November 25, 2013 at the Economist Conference, 'Cyprus on the Mend?', when she summarised the modest achievements to date that related to the immediate resolutions and recapitalisation of the Bank of Cyprus (and Hellenic Bank, the third largest) boasting that no taxpayers money had been utilised: the formula that had underpinned the whole rescue package/programme in the first place; ergo reinforcing this as a precedent to be followed in the future. The government received cautious praise for conducting prudent fiscal policies, whilst admitting to the financial hardship these policies inflicted at the conference.

This speech can only be interpreted as an upbeat message for the patient to continue their course of medicine; whatever symptoms or side effects experienced. It did not address how SME growth (the backbone of the economy) could be improved without access to the liquidity and bank credit that had previously been in surfeit. As with Greece, progress was defined within the closed walls of austerity, with authorities postulating debt reduction whilst admitting the continual need to re-evaluate forecasts.[42]

The focus by the EU and IMF on reducing the banking sector did not extend to professional services for which Cyprus had a strong tradition in legal, accounting and management consultancy. Tourism was paraded as a panacea and motor for growth: as were new potential revenue streams from the exploitation of fossil fuels in Cypriot territorial waters. This will be discussed in more detail in Chapter 5: suffice it to say that the existing business model for this required radical changes to remain competitive in a global market.

Apart from any losses sustained by the levy, many property owners were affected by plunging property prices. This was widespread in the EU generally to the extent it was no different to what was happening in Spain and Portugal (also in the UK for that matter). While the situation was aggravated by the banking crisis, it was compounded by property owners being unable to meet mortgage payments: as many had taken out risky Swiss franc denominated loans where currency fluctuations played havoc on their ability to pay resulting in massive default, although it was argued that these loans were competitive at the time.[43] Selling their properties or even renting was also made near impossible in the worsening economic climate.

Blame for this ill fortune was widely levelled on industry professionals who had encouraged and profited from the earlier boom: advisers, real estate agents and banks that advised and offered non euro loans – which mortgagors alleged were in breach of EU disclosure rules, and warnings given by the Cyprus Ministry of Finance. This led to accusations of mis-selling that many believed they had been 'mis-sold' the Swiss franc loans at the time. A substantial property owner and investor, who does not wish to be named, pointed out that 'Without adherence to government warnings given by the Ministry of Finance to banks that loans other than euro loans were not suitable for domestic use as they were complex and unstable.' Making matters worse was the fact that the banks knew, under EU law, that they could chase assets in default of loan payments across national borders – exposing property owners to seizure of assets in the UK and elsewhere in the EU. Once source from the industry, who wishes to remain anonymous, says 'the attitude of the UK Treasury was that it was nothing to do with them and that it would be a matter for the courts.'[44]

In the aggrieved climate of this downturn, class actions lawsuits by disgruntled owners against their lenders and advisors became commonplace: the first of which – representing 100 litigants – has received an undisclosed settlement by the banks to avoid a High Court judgment raising expectations for even bigger class actions in the pipeline.[45]

Some of the more breath-taking stories of financial loss relate to Cypriot expatriates recently returning to their roots to retire – many as part of the earlier tax amnesty – and bringing with them the collected earnings from business ventures in the UK or elsewhere, only to see these savings stripped away by the bail-in. In one case a business man (who wishes to remain anonymous), returning to Cyprus after decades of working in the City in London, deposited a seven figure sum euros in Laiki bank but also took out a separate loan of circa €2,000,000 for a business venture. The impact of the bail-in for him as a Laiki client was that he lost his deposits *less* the insured element – a paltry 2.5% of the total – but not the liabilities that arose from the loan. This left him with a negative balance of almost two million euros to pay. His savings now wiped out, he had to use the sum protected in the deposit account as an offset against the continued loan obligations. In another case, where those affected wish to remain anonymous, the joint account holders with €3,000,000 salvaged only €200,000 as the insured element in their case, the status of 'joint' meaning that the exemption to the levy applied simply as individuals.

Stories of such substantial losses amongst people who had nothing to do with eastern oligarchs are numerous, and many more were recorded by the authors of this book. Antoniou spelt out the fears and sense of insecurity felt by people as a consequence of what was perceived to be a harsh austerity package.

> We would have no means to support our needs anyway, we wouldn't be able to pay for petrol, pharmaceuticals, for anything, for food imports.... The economy is totally reliant on imports, so there were high fears, and these fears created insecurity and in these levels of insecurity no one would give anything to anyone unless they received cash.

In particular, he equated his feelings of the crisis with 1974:

> I was ten years old at the time of the Turkish invasion and it felt exactly the same but no obvious victims of bloodshed at the time. Others also gave the analogy of the Turkish invasion for the degree of fear and insecurity arising from this calamity in the island's short history since independence.[46]

The Troika had been against pensions used as collateral for the Cypriot contribution of €5.8 billion towards the bailout. For her part, Chancellor Merkel opposed any plans that would utilise pensions in this way as anathema to the social principles of the EU.[47] 'We want Cyprus to remain in the eurozone', she was quoted as saying – but without the business model that Cyprus appeared not to have yet abandoned. This statement reinforced the view that pensions were 'off limits'. As a senior parliamentary source said, 'Actually the pensions funds were some of the few deposits the EU accepted they would cover to some degree... they cover civil servants and they have got to keep their pensions.' This was not the experience of private sector workers drawing on their own independent pensions plans. 'There are people that were not civil servants who did not have a pension fund just savings in the bank... and *that* money came from a pension plan and they lost everything.' Michalis Antoniou echoed this view highlighting the distinction between the public and private sector pensions – particularly, in the latter case, for those without state-funded pension schemes who had been saving for retirement, and saw the bulk of that capital go up in smoke with the 'haircut' scheme:

> Someone decided that the money that people had collected throughout the years and savings just disappeared... there are people that were not civil servants who did not have a pension fund just had savings in the bank that lost everything and that money came from pension planning and they lost everything.[48]

This contrast between public and private was admittedly not absolute. In the public sector, the pension rules were rewritten much less favourably for new recruits. Under the new scheme, people recruited to the civil service (which includes teachers) from October 2010 would not receive a lump sum. Instead, they were to make direct contributions to receive their social insurance pension – as with anyone working in the private sector.[49]

## The Piraeus Asset Transfer

Aside from any of the other controversies about the banking levy, a myriad of issues surround the disposal of the Greek branches of Laiki and the Bank of Cyprus. Between them, these branches represented around 10% of the total Greek banking sector. The Troika made it a precondition for the rescue package that they were split off and sold as part of the rescue deal.[50] But the process by which this was carried out leaves a number of substantially unanswered questions.[51]

What we do know is that on March 26, 2013, Piraeus Bank became Greece's second largest lender after confirming that it had completed the acquisition of the Greek branches units of the Bank of Cyprus, Cyprus Popular Bank (Laiki) and Hellenic Bank for just over half a billion euros.[52] The sale of the Cypriot branches to Piraeus was a precondition by the Troika for the approval of Cyprus' aid package, according to Demetriades.[53] Sources close to the bank explained there had not been any serious interest by the National Bank of Greece to participate, and in the case of Alpha Bank it was suggested that they were only interested in the branches and not the employees.

The agreement meant they acquired all of the Greek deposits, loans and branches of Bank of Cyprus, Cyprus Popular Bank (CPB) and Hellenic Bank, including loans and deposits of their Greek subsidiaries (leasing, factoring and the Investment Bank of Greece (IBG), for a total cash consideration of €524 million.[54] This was despite their combined value typically being placed at around €4 billion. The measures cannot be explained as a healthy financial institution salvaging the parts of its sicker cousins – as, for example, when Barclays gobbled up the prime trading assets of Lehman in September 2008, as it went under.[55] Instead, the ECB stress tests of 2011 show that Piraeus had an exposure to Greek sovereign debt of 271% of its Tier 1 capital. This was a bank with double the exposure to Greek bonds of all the Cypriot banks combined.[56] And yet the term 'casino banking', so eagerly applied by leading EU commentators to the Cypriot owners of Greek debt, appears to have been magnanimously waved in reference to this particular institution.

The result of this extraordinary measure was that a capital deficiency of €2.7 billion was transformed into a net balance of close to €1 billion – in other words, Cypriot depositors received a haircut in order to directly recapitalise an insolvent Greek bank. Piraeus insisted in a statement about the takeover that, 'the transaction ensures the stability of the Greek banking system, provides assistance to Cyprus in relation to the resolution of the crisis and secures depositors, customers and employees of the three Cypriot banks in Greece post recent uncertainty.'[57] What assistance Cyprus received by a major capital transfer from the pockets of its own banks was left unclear.

Perhaps most controversially, Piraeus also noted that the takeover spared these branches of the formerly Cypriot banks from the banking levy: 'Customer deposits with the Greek branches of bank of Cyprus, Cyprus Popular Bank (CPB) and Hellenic Bank are not subject to any bank levy or haircut that has been agreed in Cyprus.'[58] Under the Troika's rescue plan, Cypriot based depositors had suffered the full impact of a levy that was substantially the result of a Greek debt liquidation deal – yet the *Greek* clients of those Cypriot banks were entirely spared its effect. The contradiction here is astonishing, and defies any coherent financial logic. It confirmed that two very different standards were in operation in the treatment of the banking sector, and clients, of these two countries. As a senior source close to the discussions says, 'The Cypriot depositors got to lose whereas the Greek depositors got to keep all their deposits as did the Greek depositors in the Cypriot branches in Greece. I am not saying we did not make mistakes, we made mistakes, we had to suffer the consequences of our mistakes and the banks made mistakes and their shareholders lost a lot of money... but different rules were applied in the case of Cyprus.'[59]

Why was it that so little was paid for the branches of these banks? What was the nature of the tender process for the purchase bids – and what procedures took place in the spirit of transparency and according to EU tender rules? Clearly it would be difficult to advance any satisfactory reasons acceptable to Cypriot depositors. None has been forthcoming. Although the details of the sale were not disclosed by Piraeus and the Hellenic Financial Stability Fund (HFSF) it was backed by the Greek and Cypriot governments and had to obtain the necessary approval of the EU competition authorities (DG for Competition).

The Troika excused this action at the time on the grounds that that the Cypriot bank branches in Greece would transfer to a 'local' lender as part of the effort to reduce the island's financial sector, and check the spread of contagion. Demetriades argued that a consequence of the bail-in would have been that the Greek branches of BOC and Laiki (now Cyprus Popular Bank) would have been impossible to reopen:

We wouldn't have the potential to impose restrictions on capital flow and a massive deposit outflow would ensue, resulting in the bank's collapse and the activation of the Deposit Protection Fund.[60]

What this meant in practice was that Cypriot banks were deliberately starved of capital to salvage their larger, more destitute neighbour. Such an approach perfectly aligns with our discussion of the Greek PSI and its consequences in the previous chapter. Exemptions were offered, exceptions granted, and concessions made to Greece that Cyprus, together with the clients of its financial system, had to then shoulder the burden for. The result was the destruction of a business model that represented 40% of the country's GDP. These were the sentiments of one anonymous senior banking source on this issue:

> A political decision was taken to protect the Greek banking system from the instability of the Cypriot banks ... All the losses were born by the Cypriot shareholders of the banks, the Cypriot bondholders and the Cypriot depositors. The Greek banking system was protected, the Cypriot banking system was completely decimated, and this was a political decision: it was not a financial decision taken by the Eurogroup of the EU.[61]

## Austerity, Banking and Housing Bubble Parallels

Ireland was the first eurozone member to experience an EU bailout for reasons that are at least comparable to those of Cyprus. Its origins lay in the overextension of bank lending to an overheated construction boom: one where property prices had risen to unsustainable levels of bank lending (growing as it did by 1200% between 1995 and 2006),[62] which fuelled a regional property and financial bubble. The surge in bad loans forced the government to provide guarantees of financial support and recapitalise the nation's three main banks. Preference shares were purchased in Allied Irish Bank, (AIB) Bank of Ireland (BOI) and Anglo Irish where the state held 75%.[63]

As both the banking and sovereign debt situation deteriorated and the 2008 guarantees expired in September 2010, the government was forced to seek an EU bailout in November of that year. The Agreement on the November 28, with the IMF and the EU secured a bailout of €90 billion for an emergency package to prop up the banks and stem fears of a wider contagion in the eurozone. The deal came with a painful austerity package of spending cuts of €18 billion to unemployment and welfare benefits. The Irish bailout 'should address the current nervousness in the financial markets', European Union Economic Commissioner Olli Rehn told reporters in Brussels.

The rescue saw the EU putting up $60 billion and the Washington-based IMF an additional $30 billion. In a statement, IMF Managing Director Dominique Strauss-Kahn said the deal would see a broad restructuring of the once spectacularly successful Irish banks, 'A fundamental downsizing and reorganisation to restore the viability of the system will commence immediately...At the end of this process, a...better capitalized banking system will emerge to effectively serve the needs of the Irish economy.'[64]

There was no hint of a 'systemic" failure of the eurozone in the case of Ireland. Its GDP was even smaller than Greece – at slightly under 6% of the region – and its sovereign debt was less widely owned. Yet the EU was still keen to stem growing concerns of investors in the bond market already worried about Portugal and Spain. The latter in particular comprised the fourth largest economy in the eurozone: meaning that the European Financial Stability Facility (EFSF) would be hard-pressed to bail the country out with its existing package of funds.

There was already a flight of capital from the Irish banks and this was escalating to crisis-prone states, and bondholders continued to be apprehensive on hearing of initiatives on how losses in the future could be distributed to them directly via the 'selective' default of another PSI. However the EU modified its tone by suggesting that this would only be the case where insolvency was at stake.

With recent memories of the way in which their own EU-funded banking rescue was handled, the Spanish press – led by the daily, *El País* – echoed the fears around the eurozone for possible future implications for depositors.[65] A clear sense of insecurity emerged following the actions against those 'uninsured' Cypriot depositors who were being punished 'Castigo en Nicosia' for their banks' failings rather than the shareholders or state. It was in fact from Spain that some of the strongest criticism and sympathy against the Cypriot bail-in conditions came: a stark reminder for Spaniards of their own banking crisis.

What went wrong in Spain and are there any parallels with the Cypriot experience? On the surface the Spanish financial regime was credited as one of the most competent to deal with the 2008–2009 liquidity freeze. Its banks operated under strictly regulated practices, relating to their *inter alia* provisions of high capital and low leverage. But as the economy bloomed during the property boom, this modus operandi began to unwind.

The explosion in residential and commercial housing development was poorly regulated and produced the biggest property bubble in Europe.[66] Its collapse led to prices plummeting by up to 40%, leaving the 'Cajas' – or regional and local savings banks – almost insolvent with distressed assets in cities and resorts all over Spain.[67] It was mainly the Cajas that had been lending very heavily to property companies that went bankrupt. The effect of this was to leave a massive loan portfolio of bad debts.

All this drew obvious comparisons with the circumstances of Cyprus. Before the global financial crisis, the Spanish government had maintained one of the eurozone's lowest debt-to-GDP ratios at 42% – when Germany's was then 66%. It offered sustained bailout relief to the Cajas through the Spanish Rescue funds (FROB - Fondo de reestructuración ordenada bancaria ) but by May 2012, with difficulty getting access to the capital markets and with the nationalisation of Bankia bank, the scene had been set for a bank rescue package.[68] There was tension between the EU and the Spanish Government, with the latter wanting the EU to recognise this as purely a banking, and not one linked to sovereign, debt crisis. A bailout was finally approved linked a bank restructuring programme for three Spanish banks in November 2012.

As with Cyprus, Spain had no resolution framework in its supervisory arsenal and had to agree to independent stress audits: much to the humiliation of the Central Bank of Spain. After meeting with his Spanish counterpart, German Finance Minister Wolfgang Schäuble insisted that there was little flexibility in the Troika's austerity conditions. 'The first precondition in order to have sustainable growth everywhere in Europe is fiscal consolidation,' Schäuble said.[69] What he did not say was that it wasn't only the Spanish banks that were heavily exposed to the property crash – other European banks that had provided loans for foreign property investments such as Deutsche Germany's Landesbanks had a combined exposure of over

€100 billion. However, Wolfgang's comments seemed to set the tone for the forthcoming negotiations between Cyprus and its eurozone partners in late 2012 and early 2013.

It is extremely popular, both in the press and political establishment, to equate the banking systems of the European financial centres of Cyprus, Malta and Luxemberg. The analogy is far from irrelevant or uninteresting, but falls short on a number of points. Essentially speaking, the Cypriot banking system was so large that the cash-strapped government was not able to meet its obligations in respect to deposit guarantees. In Cyprus the ratio of deposits to GDP stood at 259% in April 2013; that is the size of the deposit base excluding the holdings of monetary financial institutions and central government. With Malta the ratio of deposits to GDP in 2013 was substantially lower (173%), and the country hosts a stronger presence of foreign banks. In terms of the assets held by the leading Maltese banks, these represent only two times GDP, which is still below the EU average. But mostly importantly, its own banks did not have to contend with the massive losses inflicted on Cyprus by the Greek PSI.

Notwithstanding this difference, there is real concern that the banking sector in Malta is still growing faster than the real economy. If the current rate of growth is maintained then within five years Malta *may* mirror the same deposit-to-GDP ratio as that of Cyprus (in 2013) – except, of course, that it would benefit from the much more international presence of its international banks.[70]

At a staggering 534% at the time of writing, Luxembourg's banks have a much higher ratio of deposits to GDP than Malta. The major difference between Luxembourg and Cyprus is the location of the 'home' base of these banks. The three largest banks in Cyprus are domestic banks – Bank of Cyprus, Laiki Bank (Cyprus Popular Bank) and Hellenic Bank – which exposed the Cyprus government to cover the deposit guarantees. This is in contrast to the position in Luxembourg, where only one of the biggest banks is a domestic bank – namely; Banque et Caisse d'Epargne de l' Etat, the other two being French owned.[71]

If the material comparison between Cyprus and its two closest European colleagues is partly lacking, the psychological impact of the bail-in is very real. The events of March 2013 showed that all eurozone politicians were anxious to restore calm in the markets. This was no more clearly seen in the remarks of the Luxembourg

Finance Minister – representing as he did a country with an oversized finance sector – when he warned that the example set in Cyprus by taxing people holding €100,000 ($129,000) or more in their accounts could drive investors out of Europe. 'This will lead to a situation in which investors invest their money outside the euro zone,' he told *Der Spiegel*. 'In this difficult situation, we need to avoid anything that will lead to instability and destroy the trust of savers.'[72]

## Cyprus and the Politicised 'Russian' Connection

We have talked at length earlier about the Russian connection, both the financialisation of Cyprus, and its public treatment by the Troika and other EU commentators. It is true that rich Russians had deposited billions of euros in Cyprus' banks and many of them were forced to share in the effects of the bail-in. The EU Commission, ECB and IMF were in absolutely no mood to exempt them; indeed, the idea of punishing the corrupting influence of 'oligarch' money was pivotal to how the levy strategy was sold to the press and people of Europe. Nevertheless, a confidential German foreign Intelligence Service report (BND) had identified that Russian Oligarchs and Russian businessmen had parked large funds, the equivalent of up to $30 billion, well in excess of the total GDP in the Republic of Cyprus in the main commercial banks (Bank of Cyprus and Laiki) but also other lesser known banks.[73,74]

Ironically, the economic problems in the eurozone may have been a lever for funds returning to Russia or other now 'safer' tax havens that were free from the grasping hand of the Troika. It is generally believed that some of the larger Russian deposits were thought to have escaped the 'haircut' as a result of alleged insider knowledge, prior to the freezing of Bank of Cyprus and Laiki bank accounts. Transfers of funds back to the mainland that had been hidden offshore were being encouraged by a tax amnesty offered by Vladimir Putin for Russians to come clean, provided any outstanding tax was paid at the amnesty rate.[75]

When the discussion of a Cyprus rescue plan among European Union leaders began to include talk of confiscating a share of deposits in Cypriot banks, Russia's leaders expressed shock and outrage. President Vladimir V. Putin called the action 'intolerable'. Prime Minister Dmitri A. Medvedev admitted that there were 'government funds' in bank accounts and described the levy as amounting to 'stealing of what has already been stolen'.[76]

The Russian government was considering a further loan to bail out Cyprus but there was no evidence of enthusiasm for it. Moscow had already given Cyprus a €2.5 billion loan in 2011, and nor had the Russian government been consulted by the EU in the talks when the plan for the levy was formulated.[77] Moscow later assessed that a full-scale rescue could cost it close to six billion euros.[78]

During the March bailout negotiations with the Troika, Finance Minister Michael Sarris flew out to Moscow to request a further loan including the refinancing of the existing one. This time no deal materialised. There were a number of reasons for the reluctance on the Russian side. Sarris suggested this about his Moscow meetings:

> The summary of the message (from his Russian counterparts) was, we helped you once on the understanding that you would take measures that would help you return to the market and that you would pay us back; you didn't and you are asking us to help you again now and our lives are complicated by the fact that it is not as easy now to lend as it was. It will particularly be seen to be helping Russian oligarchs (they said)...you know the internal politics of Russia is changing also.

The disappearance of Russia from the political scene in Cyprus in 2013 also, effectively, gave the Troika a free hand in the negotiations. As he points out:

> ...they (the Russians) were clearly under pressure from the EU not to meddle in family affairs. The family being the EU and the Russians having been, how can I put it, the unwelcome opportunity to come in again. They were accused by the EU of interfering...but at the same time we (the EU) are allowed to impose draconian conditions, and as part of the draconian decisions we are going to take a pair of heavy scissors against all your depositors...it's amazing!

Sarris went on to say:

> ...if they really had good will (the EU) they would have said to the Russians, think seriously about capitalising one of the banks,

because that way you are not lending money to *Cyprus*, but you are buying a bank. On previous occasions the Russians had an interest in Laiki Bank but they were not ready to assume the risk of Greece going out of the euro to the drachma. Yes, during 2012 when I was chairman of Laiki Bank during the first six months I made a very concerted effort to interest the Russians. Then I realised, without Greece and dealing with the Greek situation it would have been impossible. I also tried to persuade the Greeks to let us carve off the Greek operations and transform them into a Greek bank. Clearly there was no appetite for that.[79]

It was thought in Moscow that if there was a run on the banks in Cyprus a far larger amount might be needed (20 to 40 billion euros) to cover depositors' withdrawals and to recapitalise the banks. Russia had a growing budget deficit of $9.2 billion and needed to provide financing for the 2014 Winter Olympics and 2018 World Cup of €30 billion and a rescue operation of this magnitude would likely have been too much. Furthermore, the government had begun a fierce rhetorical attack on corruption, which at least in image terms would not co-ordinate well with a bailout of Cyprus.

If Russia took greater control over Cyprus's financial system it would not necessarily gain a sufficient political clout in the eurozone. This undoubtedly would be a contributory factor in the failure of negotiations in Moscow. There was even talk of bailing Cyprus out a second time in exchange for granting Gazprom, the Russian state-controlled oil giant, rights for exploration of offshore gas fields around the island. But this was made less attractive by the complications raised by the oil fields being in waters claimed by Turkey.[80] Conversely, the country is not financially dependent on Europe, and does not suffer directly from the debt, banking and contagion concerns of the region. Direct foreign investment into Russia does not come from the heart of the European Union, but more often than not from offshore territories and tax havens. Germany, by contrast, accounted for just 4 per cent of foreign direct investment in Russia.

# 5
# Economic Recovery and Strategic Challenges

## Banking Confidence and the Eurozone

Following the financial crash of 2008, European nations have been busy restructuring and rebalancing their economies, with varying success. Substantial sovereign and bank debt led the eurozone to fall into a prolonged recession in 2011 as the extent of its problems became fully apparent. This is in contrast to the far stronger growth rates being seen in the United Kingdom and the USA. Furthermore, deflation is now a severe and rising threat to the entire eurozone. The question has been ceaselessly asked since 2010 of whether, how, and in what form the region can survive. Since then the mood for an 'austerity' based rescue programme has changed dramatically, and the effectiveness of this approach in achieving real growth and debt recovery in the eurozone is even being questioned by the IMF – its proponent for financial crises around the globe for decades. Proposals are increasingly looking at how to avoid future government bailouts, and so save their costs from falling on the shoulders of taxpayers. In Greece, as in other bailout eurozone states, the tax burden is being felt mostly by the public sector and other salaried employees, where income tax is taken at source. Cyprus was, of course, advocated as an alternative approach – where the taxpayer would avoid shouldering the costs of the rescue package, at least directly.

Economists have long been familiar with a concept known as 'moral hazard' – a scenario that creates incentive for individuals to act recklessly by insulating them from the consequences of their actions. By insuring risk, governments create perverse incentives that make banks less cautious and less willing to appropriately price such risk. In the Cypriot case, instead of the banks making effective provisions in the event of financial trouble, the government assured cheap credit, backed by low interest rates and the supportive financial structure of the EU and then the eurozone. The about-turn in the fortunes of those banks that resulted from the Greek PSI, an almost unthinkable event before the European debt crisis, and the resulting, unprecedented, confiscation of private accounts gives the implications of moral hazard a whole new dimension. The novel manoeuvre to save Cyprus punished the country for its economic ties to Greece, and depositors for holding large savings accounts.

A wider point must be raised here. Confidence in the banking system is fundamentally a self-fulfilling prophecy. If people believe their deposits are safe, stable, and calm, then they will be – which justifies their confidence in the security of deposits in the first place. This faith is the cornerstone on which a fractional reserve system depends. But the logic applies equally well in the opposite direction; when the collapse in such confidence threatens any banks affected with default, or an eponymous 'bank run'. Such were the lessons learnt in the Great Depression, especially in the US, when between 1930 and 1933 the banking system shrank by half. Without a government guarantee of deposits, people hoarded money – this, coupled with the collapse of banks, played a major role in the reduction of the money supply, and the deflationary spiral that intensified the Depression, if not producing the worst of its effects.[1]

State institutions therefore play a crucial role in maintaining and generating such confidence. The government, national or federal, provides a variety of 'deposit guarantee' schemes to maintain public confidence in the banking system, even in the highly unlikely event of a bank failure. An extreme example of this was the nationalisation of Northern Rock in February 2008 by the British Labour Government, the culmination of a process whereby it pledged to guarantee all saver deposits in the bank in September 2007, after a run on it that month led to over £2 billion being withdrawn in the space of weeks. This was explicitly after private bids had been unable to absolutely guarantee depositor savings.[2] Aside from the role of government in this process is that of central banks, including increasingly the ECB, as 'lenders of last resort'.[3] Such banks provide potentially unlimited, though highly conditional, liquidity schemes to maintain the solvency of the banking system, by ensuring public confidence in it.

The potential for a Cyprus-style crisis to undermine such confidence is not hard to see. At the very least, if this was to be a model for further bail-out rescues no depositors would wish to hold accounts above 100k of euros in eurozone banks. The Savings and Loans debacle of the 1990s in the United States during the Reagan presidency had taught depositors the importance of maintaining deposits in separate accounts only up to the 'insured protected levels' for state compensation purposes.[4] Non-eurozone member states have their own approaches to this – in the UK, deposits are insured against bank failure for up to £85K (€100K equivalent) under the UK financial protection scheme, so diligent depositors know to spread their assets accordingly. At the same time, the UK Government did not impose a haircut on bank depositors when RBS and Lloyds had to be rescued in the fall of 2008, or Northern Rock a year earlier. The bail-out in the UK did see shareholder values plunge in the distressed banks – but this was the product of market forces, not engineered by governmental authorities as part of the haircut on shareholders.

EU Commissioner Olli Rehn admitted there had been 'mistakes' in the handling of Cyprus – implicitly noting how even ordinary depositors had no protection in the handling of the process. Looking to the future of EU policy he concluded that they must draw two key lessons from the crisis. Firstly was the need for an 'absolute clarity about secured deposits' – taking into account that this brief threat to take the savings of small investors not only created panic in Cyprus but elsewhere in Europe – until of course the bail in terms were altered/changed. The second lesson comes from the remarks in the Commissioner's statement: ' ... the developments in Cyprus demonstrate the reasons why a Banking Union is a necessary element of a true EMU. We need a well-functioning Single Supervisory Mechanism with a single rulebook to prevent the emergence of an unsustainable banking sector like in Cyprus ... we must ensure that even if the reinforced supervision fails, we have a Single Resolution Mechanism to provide the instruments for a timely and effective restructuring and resolution of the problem banks.[5]

## The Rapid Recovery of Cyprus

In terms of the recovery path since March 2013, Cyprus has proven to be a very different case to its closest neighbour, Greece. Indications are that the financial crisis seems to be under control, and there are strong suggestions in the economic data to show that the worst may soon be over. The pace of economic recovery has been far more rapid than was generally expected – especially when compared with other eurozone bailouts. One politician remarked that, 'This is still the most serious recession since the Turkish invasion in 1974, but it has been less severe than anticipated.'[6] The Cypriot economy did not shrink by 20% after the banks collapsed last March, as some feared. It did not even shrink by 8.7%, as the Troika had expected. The final figure for 2013 came in at 5.4%. In May 2014, it was being reported that the Troika had lowered their expectations on the depth of recession to 4.2%, from a February projection of 4.8%. Although Cyprus' economy contracted by 5.4% in 2013, this was 3% less than forecast and on this basis the Troika (with the IMF) were estimating a return to growth of about 0.4% in 2015.[7] These estimates were also backed up by Ernst and Young.[8]

The EU–IMF team has for once been confounded by success after vastly underestimating the damage of austerity in a string of countries. For obvious reasons, the IMF wants to attribute this to success of the 'bail-in' experiment. The evidence for this, however, is thin – as are their claims for being responsible for the Greek return to growth in 2014. There are better grounds for explaining this; namely, a number of fundamental economic positives, and important structural reforms.

The evidence is clear that Cyprus should nudge its way out of recession and into positive growth in 2015, with the indicators showing that the rate of unemployment, although still above 15%, is at least stabilising.[9] This recovery is being helped substantially by the readoption of elements of the business model that was developed in the wake of the 1974 invasion, and was based on cultivating new tourist venues after the loss of the northern coastline and

Famagusta resort district. As one source from the government, who wished to remain anonymous, pointed out, 'We built a healthy tourism sector for about 10–20 years but then came financial services that did not create real investments in production. A lot of money was going around but we never tackled our growth model like Ireland with real growth, real investment, real productive activities, with one of the lowest corporation taxes in Europe.'[10] It also helps that the country elected a no-nonsense government that is abiding strictly to the terms of the EU–IMF memorandum. Says Minister of Finance Harris Georgiades at a meeting in Brussels in December 2013, 'We're aligned with the Troika .... The memorandum could have been our own manifesto. It's a chance to correct our own shortcomings, and do what should have been done in Cyprus long ago.' At the same time, he acknowledged that 'the Cypriot government accepted the bail-in under duress', and that the 'absence of an adequate framework' surrounding such a policy produced a measure of 'side-effects and repercussions.'[11] Such a careful, moderate statement of reflection earmarks a general policy to diffuse recriminations and blame for the eventual outcome of the negotiations. It is reflecting of the approach by the establishment in general to handling the crisis and its consequences and moving on rapidly. Cypriots speak Greek – and can claim to be part of the Hellenic diaspora – but the political atmosphere of the island is a far cry from the tumult of Athens – where the Leftist, anti-austerity party SYRIZA leads the polls with a vow to tear up Greece's memorandum, and Golden Dawn fascists are on patrol. There is a broad acceptance and understanding of what went wrong. This was poignantly expressed by Georgiades, stating inter alia that, 'The problems of the Cypriot economy are essentially self-sustained.' He went on to explain that

> The problems are twofold. They relate on the one hand to a rather inefficient and wasteful public sector. Over the years public spending was rising more than the growth of the economy. The public sector wage bill became proportionately the largest in the EU. Critically, during the last few years public spending kept rising even as public revenues were, in fact, falling. Public debt was rising rapidly before even a euro was used to recapitalise banks.

He went on to refer to the banks as being the second problem:

> Whilst the public sector was over-spending the private sector was over-borrowing. Lending was offered not so much on the basis of well thought out business plans but simply on the basis of collateral. The banking system was financing not so much real investment but, rather, consumption and a property bubble.[12]

While acknowledging these causes, the minister was able to report significant progress in the financial sector towards the process of recapitalisation. In particular, he offered confirmation of the implementation of much needed restricting plans in both the banking and public sector, and was able to announce structural reforms to the civil service, welfare and healthcare, as well as a programme of privatisation to encourage inward investment.

As early as November 25, 2013, the head of the IMF Cyprus team, Delia Velculescu, was able to claim at a speech at the Economist Conference: 'Much has been accomplished within a relatively short time since the approval and start of the stability programme for Cyprus.' In her address she highlighted that the two largest and insolvent banks were resolved and merged, while Hellenic bank was recapitalised with €100 million euros by the investment of three private investors in exchange for a 75% capital position in the bank. It had always been a proud statement of the lenders that taxpayer money had not been used in this bail-out and the speech did not fail to mention it again, with Velculescu emphasising that, 'No taxpayer money was used in the process. This allowed for broader burden sharing of costs and prevented an otherwise unsustainable increase in public debt.' While this is true in the technical sense, it does not discuss the knock-on effect for ordinary citizens with respect to welfare and job losses, meaning that taxpayers were hardly spared the 'costs' of the rescue package.

The speech also made extensive reference to the efforts to sort out the pension system, a particular concern of the Troika during the negotiations prior to the signing of the MoU and Stability Pact, and she remarked on their progress: '...to restore the sustainability of the pension system and strengthen the economy's competitiveness, key structural reforms were implemented early on, including to the pension system and the COLA wage indexation mechanism. Some results can already be seen: a recent review of the pension system confirmed its long-run viability; and there are signs that the downward wage flexibility is helping to cushion jobs.'[13]

As part of the conditions of implementation, the Troika continues to monitor the Cypriot economic temperature with formal visits to measure progress and financial health. Quarterly assessments are prepared against the criteria laid down in the European Stability Mechanism's (ESM) programme for Cyprus. Progress reports by the Troika state that it remains on track:

> Fiscal targets for the first quarter of 2014 were met with a considerable margin, reflecting better than projected revenue performance and prudent budget execution. Progress has been made with the recapitalisation and consolidation of the cooperative credit sector, and banks are advancing with their restructuring plans.[14]

Although this covers fiscal reform and continued work in restructuring the banking sector, the privatisation of key sectors remains very much on the 'to do' list. This is as well as the implementation of measures in the banking sector to bring down the level of Non-Performing Loans (NPL), under foreclosure laws, which at 140% of GDP are the highest in Europe.

Considerable efforts are being put into improving arrears management. A new insolvency framework is in preparation to provide the right incentives for borrowers and lenders to find constructive solutions for dealing with NPLs. A Troika team is reviewing the new insolvency framework (for both corporate and personal insolvency) with the Cypriot government. The framework, which is intended to protect vulnerable groups of mortgagors from foreclosure, is expected now to be ready from early 2015.[15] A task force was established to study the title deeds issues, and the banks are working to improve their due diligence procedures as a measure to avoid and reduce the level of NPLs. This approach to assessing the creditworthiness of potential borrowers is now based on the formula of ability to pay; contrasted to the approach during the low-interest boom, where the tendency was to look at the value of the asset to be secured against a loan.

The need for an efficient public healthcare (NHS) was formally put on the table in the MoU as part of measures to deal with the inequalities in access to care, and inefficient allocation and utilisation of resources. Cyprus is the only country in the EU where the public and private sectors are split 50:50 in size compared with the average of 75:25 in favour of the public sector (with compulsory health care contributions from all those working in the public sector/elsewhere. The timetable for implementation of a form of national health service is by the end of 2015, with detailed plans for this to be monitored by the Troika at its regular review meetings in 2014. Central to the reforms is the creation of a system of family doctors or GPs as the basis of primary care to be made available to all and as the first point of contact. This proportion needs to get closer to the average of 25.5% for the European Union as a whole.

The position of tourism as a vehicle for growth was highlighted in the MoU 'as an important export sector and domestic value added and employment.'[16] Recommendations were given on strengthening the competiveness of the sector in the Mediterranean and worldwide – an issue the Cyprus Tourism Organisation (CTO) had already been addressing with initiatives based on a comprehensive strategy of increasing and upgrading the tourism offers with reduced reliance on the high seasonal 'mass market' tourism of the previous two decades. As with other popular destinations in the Mediterranean, Cyprus has struggled to 'stretch' the tourism season beyond the high and shoulder periods of the year, but both the CTO and private enterprises have worked to develop a high quality product through special interest products with agro-tourism and cultural, sport, rural, and non-motorised activities linked to responsible and sustainable products. Angelos Loizou, the chairman of the Cyprus Tourist Organisation (CTO) when addressing the House Finance Committee during the debate on the CTO budget for 2014 voiced the concern of tour operators regarding the strength of the euro particularly with regard to the inbound Russian (and Ukrainian) sector – although it affects also UK and other non-eurozone tourists. However, he gave an upbeat message regarding the organisation's new strategy to promote Cyprus as a tourist destination, indicating that the strategy is long-term. 'We are discussing everything on a 3-year basis, with airlines and tour operators.'[17]

Data from the WTC shows that the direct contribution of tourism to GDP was €1.136 billion, representing 6.8% of the total, in 2013. But the total contribution of travel and tourism to GDP was EUR 3,443.6mn (20.6% of GDP) in 2013, and is forecast to rise by 7.4% in 2014, and again by 5.1% pa to €6,067.7mn (30.9% of GDP) in 2024. In employment terms, the industry supports directly and indirectly 76,643 jobs – or 22.1% of the workforce – and this could rise substantially to 118,000 jobs and a third of the workforce by 2024.[18] As the sector is so labour intensive, it can play a significant role in reducing unemployment particularly for those seeking work for the first time and so help to meet EU targets.

Investment in infrastructure has been stepped up with the construction of prestigious marinas and golf courses as part of a diversification programme into the high-end tourism market. It will be difficult to rival Portugal and Spain with long-established popular golf and marina resorts – not least because of the longer flight times from Western European destinations. However, what Cyprus can offer is a longer high and 'shoulder' season owing to its privileged climate in the Eastern Mediterranean coupled with its proximity to the Middle East.

The growth of 'Special Interest Tourism' is a key development to capture the growing conference and meetings and incentives markets. Increasingly the island has proven a popular venue for weddings and honeymoon trips, and will look to expand special wine tours and gastronomic experiences based on religious and seasonal events following the examples of well-established locations in Central Europe, both medical and wellness tourism have been enhancing their range of offers. This is in line with the overall policy of expanding its reach to a wider international audience, with less reliance on North-West Europe where tourist arrivals have declined in favour of the expanding Russian market. Third age or 'grey' tourism is a focus encouraged by the EU to enhance low season tourism in Europe on which Cyprus is able to capitalise with its mild winters.

The completion of the new terminal at Larnaca International airport in 2011 with the upgrade of facilities at Paphos has helped to create the important 'brand' image for travellers, particularly those visiting Cyprus for the first time. The continued upgrading of existing hotels in the 3–5 star categories, as well as new and varied accommodation in smaller resorts will support tourism initiatives by local and regional councils taking ownership, a trend that is being encouraged throughout Europe.

There is a growing belief among tourism professionals that local residents can help to influence the kind of 'sustainable' and responsible tourism that can be seen as important in protecting the natural and human environment. It has a positive influence on maintaining the cohesion of local communities and increasing overall local and regional commercial and social activity, as well as a positive impact on the quality of life of local residents in the development of social and cultural activities. One important consequence for Cyprus would be if policy makers take more account of local community needs in regard to the employment and skills agenda and to creating sustainable tourism products to help sustain a viable local and regional tourism industry for the future.

The combination of these reforms and changes, coupled with the continued weakening of the euro could help to revive both tourism and the stagnant property market. For the present, the tourism sector is holding up, representing just short of 7% of GDP with the Russian market increasing by 28% to 610,00. With the revival of the UK market, the growth in passenger numbers resulting from more budget airlines the future looks promising for the industry. This kind of interest is far from confined to the UK. Cyprus has attracted Chinese inward investment. Leading this is the Hong Kong based China Glory National Investment group, who have signed with the government and the Paphos authorities an investment deal to build a golf resort at an estimated value of €1.5 billion.

Progress on the privatisation of Cyprus Airways (93.67% government-owned as of 2014) will produce a number of important scenarios. Firstly, it would be one of the components helping to meet the privatisation strategy 'encouraged' (on an advised, rather than conditional basis) in the MoU, and relieve the airline of government financial support which is presently under scrutiny by the European Commission for possible breaches of EU state aid rules.[19] A number of airlines recently made expressions of interest for the purchase of the airline. Ryanair, for example, as Europe's biggest budget carrier – with greater efficiencies and low operating costs – could help to boost tourism by making Cyprus as a destination more price competitive, thereby helping to boost tourist arrivals.

The success of the industry lies in continued investment in training to enhance skills – particularly those like 'customer care', which are associated with enhancing the tourism experience. In this capacity, the EU provides ESF social funds to address the Skills and Employability agenda as well as support to tourism SMEs through additional structural funds such as European Regional Development Funding (ERDF), which provide support for experts to help eligible companies to develop and grow their businesses, with the ultimate aim of increasing and upskilling the work force. Now that the euro has been falling substantially in value against the world's leading currencies, Cyprus, as with the other climate-friendly members of the eurozone, has an opportunity to become extremely competitive as a tourism destination.

Apart from the range and quality of the tourism offer, Cyprus needs to get its UK market back to the relative position it held before the 2008 global recession: a position damaged in its competitiveness by the relative strength of the euro, and tarnished in image by the property title deeds scandal. Many expatriate Britons (and other nationalities) that had moved to Cyprus or purchased holiday homes discovered that they had not received title deeds for their newly purchased property – in many cases, questions arose as to whether they legally owned the property at all, as some developers still had mortgages on the land. In nearly all the cases, however, the problem lay simply in the administrative delays at the overloaded Land Registry Office. The government has made it clear that the backlog will be dealt with and recognises that legislation needs to be in place to make the whole administrative process more efficient including measures for eliminating delays in litigation to streamline the whole process of registration.[20]

Cyprus is not out of the woods yet. The IMF says Cyprus faces a decade-long debt purge, with the jobless rate hitting 19.8% in 2015, and no guarantee of success at the end. Public debt is expected to peak at a ratio of 126% of GDP in 2015, but it could exceed 170% if things go wrong. 'Public debt sustainability remains vulnerable to shocks,' the IMF said. External debt is still 350% of GDP. Cypriot bank deposits have shrunk from $70bn to $47bn, and are still contracting. The IMF says bad loans of the banking system have reached 46%. Moody's says the banks will need an extra €1.2bn in capital beyond the €2.5bn set aside. Internal capital controls are being lifted, but external controls will remain, leaving Cyprus in a form of financial limbo. All money in accounts before the trap door shut in March 2013 remain frozen. Fresh deposits since March are free, creating a two-tier system. A black market has arisen to play the arbitrage game. Russians trying to get their money out can swap for new deposits for a 30% fee. Some of them have been selling the shares to distressed-asset funds at a little more than 10% of last year's bail-in value. Additionally, Cyprus' Central bank has told Bank of Cyprus to ramp up capital ahead of the 2014–15 asset quality review and stress test by the ECB. Consequently the bank has raised $1.3 billion through a share sale to private equity investors and the European Bank for Reconstruction and Development, amongst others. They bought the shares for $0.32 apiece, compared to the $1.34 the depositors were forced to pay last year.

If one goal of the Troika was to shrink Cyprus' financial service sector, it has failed. Few companies have left. There were 1,454 fresh registrations in January, bringing the total to 273,000. George Pantelides, Head of Consulting Services for Deloitte in Cyprus, said he is still recruiting large numbers of people this year. 'We were strong in financial services before the banking boom and an important international centre for commerce and trade. We operate an English legal common law system which is important for all our international clients and provide our services good value at competitive prices.'[21] Companies use Cyprus as a holding venue to list shares in London, or issue Eurobonds. That has not stopped. A fresh wave of business is arriving as Noble Energy, ENI, and Total eye the giant natural gas fields of the Eastern Mediterranean.

It didn't matter whether the Russian money was illegal or not, the 'non-EU depositors' were forced to take a substantial haircut. At Bank of Cyprus, the country's biggest financial institution, 47.5% of deposits above the insured amount of €100,000 were converted into the bank's shares. More than a third of the deposits were frozen for six, nine and twelve months without interest. The curbs Cyprus introduced on capital movement forced Wargaming.net, a videogame developer from Belarus with over 3000 employees, to buy a large stake in Cyprus' second biggest bank, Hellenic, so as to retain control over its deposits. Russians also make up a third of the Bank of Cyprus board – they include Vladimir Strzhalkovsky, the former KGB agent, who received a $100 million golden parachute when he quit as chief executive of mining giant Norilsk Nickel, the largest payout in Russian corporate history.[22]

Both before and after the Crimea annexation and unrest in the Ukraine, Russians have been second-class financial citizens of the EU. It has used them, as well as other wealthy eurozone outsiders, as guinea pigs to test the bail-in procedure – now an accepted arm of the EU's bank-rescue policy. Arguably, Europe will still be somewhat safer for Russian capital than Russia itself, where, under President Vladimir Putin, it ultimately and finally belongs to the state. But the Cypriot precedent confirms that a person's savings are no longer private property; but, potentially, a political tool to be used by governments to accomplish their goals.

More generally, the crisis in the Ukraine is not only having damaging political repercussions for the EU in its relations with Russia but severe economic ones. Sanctions against Russia have inflicted harm in both directions as the economies of Eastern Europe lose many of their traditional export markets. Although Germany only has 3.5% of its export business with Russia (not large in itself) but many German companies have investments with East European firms that also trade heavily with Russia so the fall in trade for Germany is felt *indirectly* as well as directly. In turn the crisis has also hit Germany's trade with its Eastern European partners, which buy around 10% of German exports. It is unlikely, however, that this will have a direct effect on Cyprus. Tourism with Russia is expected to grow, despite the very public and deliberate blow to depositors from that corner of the world.

In the end, the overall damage of the Cyprus crisis probably didn't exceed 1% of Russia's GDP, although, as with other EU and foreign companies doing business in Cyprus, there would be problems; not least of meeting employee payroll and operating capital to run their operations. For some years, wealthy Russians have been buying up European real estate — turning some of London's prime sectors into foreign-owned enclaves — and more than three million Russians now have European Union residency permits, which gives them an exit strategy should the increasingly volatile political situation at home turn sour. Russian elites remain understandably nervous, and continue to move their assets around into tax havens in locations perceived as politically safe. Such behaviour has made them an easy target for moralising criticism. But how different are they in this respect from the many EU citizens who, even if they don't carry the tainted label of 'oligarch', continue to park assets away from the prying eyes of their domestic authorities. Monaco, Luxemburg, the Channel Islands and the Isle of Man, not to mention the Caribbean islands, all provide more than exotic holidays for countless wealthy Europeans.

With increased globalisation and the pressure within the EU to harmonise tax regimes to provide a more level playing field – not only in the eurozone but also in all the EU member states – Russian money may be forced to look elsewhere, but until that time comes it will continue to flow into the coffers of banks offering high interest rates and the safety of protective legislation which secures their investments. Pointing fingers at the Russian money in Cyprus is rich coming from those who know full well their own houses are not in order. London is the global centre of tax avoidance and evasion – providing a natural harbour for those escaping their tax obligations in their countries of domicile, but where their property rights are more secure than at 'home' in the former USSR, China or the Third World.

What the Russian business and political class have learned from the Cypriot crisis is that their money and power cannot influence European decision makers, even when it comes to saving a small Mediterranean island from insolvency. In this way it confirms how small a political voice Russia now has within the European Union. Given this dynamic, it would be much more productive for Russia to get closer to Europe rather than stay away from it — and the pressure from Russian businesses on the government to do so will likely grow.

It is only because EU and eurozone treasuries are looking for new ways to balance their domestic welfare budgets that increasing tax revenues by clamping down on loopholes and tax havens have become more important – especially as this also requires substantial international cooperation and regulation to effectively enforce. Governments complain that tax regimes are not on level playing fields, for example in respect of corporation taxes, where one country – a well-known example being Ireland – can attract business with lower levels than neighbouring jurisdictions. In Cyprus this was done through attractive interest rates as well as low corporation taxes. How different is that from Luxemburg where billions are stashed away from the German taxman, not to mention Ireland, Latvia and other havens?

## Natural Gas and the Strategic Conflict with Turkey

Parallel to the mounting economic disaster of the eurozone has been the discovery arguably the greatest natural economic boon Cyprus has ever seen. In late 2011, Noble Energy, a leading offshore drilling contractor for the *oil and gas* industry (and listed on the New York Stock Exchange) found an estimated 142 to 227 billion cubic meters of gas off the south-eastern coast of Cyprus. The huge gas fields span both Cyprus' and Israel's territorial waters. The company has subsequently found around four to six trillion cubic feet (TCF) of natural gas in a single bloc of the Aphrodite field to the south of the island, prompting statements from the government's foreign minister Mr Kasoulides to claim that there will be enough to change the island's long-term economic prospects, and to fully pay off the EU €10bn bailout rescue package.[23] Some officials are estimating that there is up to 60 trillion cubic feet of gas still to be discovered, and 1.7 billion barrels of crude oil.

After discovering such significant reserves, the Cyprus Government confirmed its intention to cooperate with Israel on drilling. This led to two Israeli firms, Delek and Anver, signing an agreement to acquire 30% of rights to explore for gas and oil off the Cyprus coastline, the drilling to be conducted by Noble Energy. Neoklis Sylikiotis, the Cyprus Minister of Commerce at the time said of the deal, described it as opening the door to a new era of Cypriot–Israeli cooperation. An agreement had also been signed with Total, France's energy conglomerate, to conduct exploratory drilling for gas and oil in Cyprus waters. Sylikiotis said that having countries such as France, the United States, Israel and Italy involved in the island's hydrocarbon exploration acted as a 'political shield' against Turkish threats.[24]

Cyprus is not a country otherwise blessed with natural resources – save an unending supply of sunshine – and the recent discoveries of natural gas have the potential to transform its fortunes at a propitious time. It also comes with its fair share of dangers. While the discovery of huge natural gas reserves off the southern coast of Cyprus represent a financial windfall, the challenges to monetise those resources are fraught with political and economic risk. It will take billions of euros required to fund an offshore pipeline and liquification plant – money the cash-strapped state cannot easily provide without massive foreign contributions.[25] As a consequence, progress has been slow, as the country has struggled to nail down the extensive financing required. But the greatest challenge may be a political one that is old and familiar to the island's history. The pipeline plans face significant opposition from the Turkish government, which has been closely monitoring the drilling operations for oil and natural gas in the exclusive economic zone (EEZ) off southern Cyprus, and has said it would oppose any attempt to pre-sell Cypriot gas before a settlement over the divided island is found.

On the flip side of the renewed possibility of prosperity lurks a profound danger. If poorly managed, Cypriot gas could harden political divisions, and intensify the lingering hostilities on the island. Turkey badly needs the region's gas to free itself from Russia's stranglehold, and has claimed the blocs to the south of Cyprus as far as Egyptian waters. Technically speaking, Ankara does not recognise the government in Nicosia, and has threatened military force if Cyprus allows drilling in the disputed maritime zone.

Turkey is no stranger to conflicts over maritime sovereignty – for years it has disputed the international rights of Greece to its own territorial waters, namely the Greek continental shelf around its northern Aegean islands. The Turkish government has expressed its concern over Greek Cyprus' 'one-sided' off-shore hydrocarbon searches, after the Turkish administration of northern Cyprus announced that a new ship had begun unilateral exploration in its 'so-called exclusive economic zone'. Turkey is keen to muscle in on this newly discovered wealth and wants any exploration to be conditional on a settlement of the political conflict. 'Turkey follows with concern the Greek Cypriot administration's continuing unilateral research activities of hydrocarbon resources in its so called exclusive economic zone without taking into account the Turkish Cypriots' detailed and concrete cooperation proposals for a fair sharing,' the Turkish Foreign Ministry said in a written statement released on the October 4, 2014. It has stated that all revenues obtained from the drilling operations off the coast of Cyprus should be distributed between Greek Cyprus and Turkish Cyprus, and have frequently warned that Turkey would undertake unilateral drilling of its own in the event of any failure to equitably share revenues. Reiterating Turkey's 'determination to maintain its constructive support', the statement also 'to prevent the provocative and unilateral steps' of

Greek Cyprus stressed the country's caution against potential reper-cussions of the Greek Cyprus' 'irresponsible act' over the ongoing peace efforts to reunify the divided island, 'which Turkey expects to have positive results soon'. Nevertheless, it emphasised that 'Turkey expects the GCA (Greek Cypriot Administration) to refrain from act-ing as if it is the sole owner of the resources of the Island, to halt its unilateral research activities and to adopt an understanding with a view to establishing a new partnership.'[26] What may also be of concern to Turkey is the realignment of Cyprus with the other natu-ral gas beneficiaries in the Eastern Mediterranean, namely Israel and Egypt – and its readiness to cooperate with NATO in the 'Partnership for Peace' initiative.

In theory, the discovery could provide a window for a historic breakthrough between Nicosia and Ankara.  This could become the catalyst not only for improving the economic prosperity of the Republic of Cyprus but for a political accommodation across the island. Indeed this may be a necessary prerequisite for the exploration phase: without political settlement, there will always be potential risks for investing companies, despite the fact they can obtain oper-ating licences to drill in government held zones of the continental shelf whose ownership is recognised in international law.

The Cypriot government has been more than receptive to this. It has to be remembered that President Anastasiades, along with his deceased predecessor Glafkos Clerides, had actually supported the Yes vote for the Annan Plan – and now there is even greater motivation to reactivate negotiations for a settlement. The administration has stated that these resources, when commercially realised, would be used for the benefit of all Cypriots, Greek and Turkish Cypriots alike: an attempt to deflect argument that drilling activities only serves the interests of citizens in the territory controlled by the *de jure* Greek government of the island.

It is too early to assess whether Cyprus could be a major player in Europe's gas supplies. Nobody knows quite how much gas there is. However, the indications are that this could be the case espe-cially as numerous exploration companies have come on board in the drilling operations (for which see below), with expectations that gas could come on stream by 2019. The discoveries by Noble so far are already extraordinary in size. Optimists say there could be 60 tril-lion cubic feet in Cypriot waters – enough to meet Europe's entire gas needs for three years (and a comparable find to the discovery of North Sea oil for Norway and Great Britain in the 1980s). The construction of a liquefied national gas plant (LNG) is being considered by the government, subject to availability of private equity finance.

Both ENI of Italy and the Chinese have shown interest in this.[27] This would remove the need for a pipeline to Turkey as a conduit to European markets. Although this would be the cheaper option, relations with Turkey would have to be put on a sound footing with no possibility of success without a political settlement. China is looking at playing a role in Cyprus' multibillion-dollar plans to develop the island's natural gas reserves, including possible investment in a liquefied natural gas (LNG) export terminal. The country is seeking to access new gas sources around the world as its energy demand rises and the government encourages industry to move to cleaner gas from coal. Cyprus hopes to attract large investors to take a stake in its gas fields, an option which a Chinese delegation is in Cyprus today to discuss. 'There is very strong interest from China . . . in energy, in the whole value chain, upstream, downstream and midstream,' Cypriot Energy Minister George Lakkotrypis said.[28] Italian energy major ENI is also interested in Cyprus' gas fields, and is set to sign a memorandum of understanding with the government over the construction of an LNG export terminal. ENI has already signed an exploration and production-sharing contract with the government to search in three offshore areas, with exploration expected to begin in the second half of this year.

Energy security and regional unity are two issues that are increasingly aligned – especially with regard to the economic engagement between the West, Russia and the Middle East. The discoveries in Cyprus, and the renewed international interest surrounding them, confirm that Cyprus remains closely plugged into the security infrastructure of the Mediterranean. 'The eastern Mediterranean has become the focus of attention for the whole world. We are in the front line of a volatile area and we are upgrading our responsibility,' said the foreign minister.[29] Cyprus has suddenly found itself the subject of more official US interest than at any point since after the 1974 invasion. Visiting the island in May of 2014, US Vice-President Joe Biden said enthusiastically upon landing at Larnaca airport, 'I wanted to come to primarily underscore the value the United States attaches to our growing cooperation with the republic of Cyprus,' and referred to a 'genuine strategic partnership which holds great promise'.

Biden's visit marks a renewed US effort to intervene in the region, pushing the two sides to renew peace talks. He is by far the most senior US official to visit Cyprus for half a century, and marks the United States' intense interest in the new potential Eldorado lying at the base of the eastern Mediterranean. With the recent events of the Ukraine in mind, the discovery has been discussed and seen in strategic. The US has also seen the merits in being proactive in bringing about a permanent political solution to the partition: as the Vice President further stated that 'an important focus of conversations' would be the settlement process itself. The Greek and Turkish Cypriot administrations have signed a document laying out the general principles of cooperation. Mr Kasoulides, the Republic's foreign minister, said this text is entirely different from the 'Annan Plan' to end the partition that was rejected by the Greek side in a referendum in 2004 soon after Cyprus had secured its place in the EU, though accepted by Turkish Cypriots. 'It talks about one country and a single sovereignty, and does not permit a legal divorce,' he said, predicting that the Greek Cypriots are likely to vote 'Yes' this time, provided there is no attempt to exploit the economic crisis to twist their arms.[30] There are a number of good reasons why this time realistic progress can be made on two fronts. Firstly, there is a greater incentive to share the benefits of the gas bonanza which could in itself be the main source of revenue in the future to help pay for the reconstruction of the occupied North's economy over time. Turkey would be 'estopped' from engaging in military threats or even intervention as this would be detrimental to the very people it claimed to protect. Clearly the fear of oil companies to invest would also be assuaged if the threat of Turkish warships disappears. With the Americans taking a serious interest, most of the ingredients for a successful settlement are present with the economic agenda driving the political one.[31] It makes this discovery a golden opportunity for all stakeholders to progress on a broad front in the interests of the island's future prosperity. It is also one which will require a mutual vision that has not been seen before. Learning from the mistakes of the past is one thing: having the courage to step away from repeating them is another.

Such progressive efforts to establish political and economic security, and peace, stand in contrast to the political damage wrought by the bail-in. In strategic terms, the EU hurt not only Cyprus and itself, but also the interests of the US and other allies in the West. Europe pushed Cyprus directly into the arms of the Russian government. Not only did this hurt the prospects for its own deal, but it gave leverage to Moscow in the process. More important still, however, by forcing Anastasiades between the rock of a forced bank levy and the hard place of seeking assistance from Moscow, the EU and the Troika seriously undermined him precisely when the West needed a strong and pro-Western Cypriot president and regime at a strategic proximity to the Middle East.

With its stable and internationally respected legal system – modelled on English common law – and strategic proximity to vital crossroads that include the Suez canal, it is not difficult to give it the title as the 'the lighthouse of the eastern Mediterranean', making it particularly attractive to countries such as Russia to try and establish port rights. Commercially as well as politically, Cyprus is the lighthouse of the eastern Mediterranean. The country has the world's tenth biggest merchant fleet, with 155 shipping companies controlling 2,300 seagoing vessels. None of these firms has left since the crisis. The shipping sector in Cyprus provided 5.1% of GDP in 2013, the highest figure since 2010, according to a survey from the Central Bank of Cyprus. Turnover rose to €417M ($655M) during the second half of 2013, up from €402M during first half. However, these figures were the lowest in four years, reflecting the country's eurozone bailout. Most revenues came from Germany ship managers (53%), followed by Vietnam (6%), Russia (5%), and Singapore (4%). About 43% of company revenue fell in a range between €1.2M and €15M, with 15% of $20.3M or more. Ship management accounted for 78% and chartering services 11% of the industry's revenues.[32,33]

No business model for the recovery can ignore the importance of the SME sector, its main driver and focus in supporting the economy. As George Pantelides stated, 'We need to support our SMEs base. These companies are the life blood of the economy. As in the rest of Europe they can be the engine of growth especially in sectors such as the hospitality and leisure. This will fundamentally contribute to the economy and specifically in providing jobs in the community especially for the young unemployed.' On the crisis itself, he offered this observation:

> Cyprus is no different from other eurozone 'bailed out' countries in being hit by the rapid increase in unemployment. Many of those laid off or have been encouraged to be benefitted from early retirement schemes in the highly affected sectors such as the banking and construction sectors are highly qualified professionals and their loss to the economy is Cyprus's loss too. Cypriot companies have to find new markets for their products beyond the internal domestic market and it is these professionals that help to support this process.[34]

# 6
# Bail-In and the Future of the Eurozone

## A Dream Undone?

This book is primarily concerned with the causes and consequences of the Cypriot financial crisis, and its place in the history of the island since independence. It is clear, however, how integrated the Cypriot story is with the wider issues at work in banking and sovereign finance: both the speculative bubble that provoked the global crisis of 2007–8 and its aftermath, and the unravelling of the eurozone as a political and economic project for prosperity. It was intimately involved in both trends, and both enjoyed and suffered the consequences. In fact, perhaps no other nation has been quite so bound up in these separate, parallel processes. Britain was and is the hub of a network of global finance, on which Cyprus was a smaller but still-important node – but the country avoided joining the eurozone, and the associated disasters that much of that region has suffered since 2009.

Some broader ideas about the direction, and future of the eurozone need to be discussed before the specific position of Cyprus, in relation to them, can be explained. Most important in connection to the story of Cyprus and the eurozone is the wider issue of the institutions of the Troika and the EU, and what their handling of the crisis suggests about the future of the region. It is worth being reminded here of the rationale for the euro's introduction; namely, that it was envisioned by its political architects as a device to create an 'island of stability' in what was increasingly seen as a volatile world with fluctuating exchange rates necessitating stable monetary policies to support economic growth.[1]

The basic idea of austerity is that too many eurozone countries have lived beyond their means for too long and now need to take responsibility for their profligacy. Budget retrenchment will ensure that countries live within their means, while the retraction of public services will make their economies leaner, fitter and more competitive. Under the watchful eye of the Troika, governments have introduced such measures by slashing welfare and infrastructure budgets: an approach which has done nothing to generate growth, and fuelled a recessionary spiral that makes the relative sovereign debt burden worse, not better. Internal devaluation in respect of wage cuts, pensions and job losses in (admittedly usually bloated) public sectors has replaced the orthodox currency devaluation of the past, and proven a poor substitute in that regard. ECB hands-off monetarist policies have overwhelmingly failed to help growth in the rest of the eurozone.

For the past eight years most of the European economies have experienced severe economic crisis, stagnation and recession – initialised by the financial crash of 2008, and exacerbated by the particular political and monetary conditions of the eurozone. In Mediterranean economies the crisis was exacerbated by the crisis of sovereign debt in general and by austerity programmes in particular. Unemployment levels have reached double digits on average in the European Union and extreme levels in the South – in excess of 25% (with youth employment standing at nearly 40% in both Greece and Spain). Under those conditions, economic growth in real terms is not possible. Cuts in welfare expenditure, wages and public employment level brought on by austerity restrictions have worsened the living conditions of people dramatically, and resulted in a severe economic contraction in much of the South. This is as public discourse about the imbalances within the eurozone characterises the divide rhetorically: as the problem of 'laziness against effort', or 'Mediterranean corruption' against the integrity and principle of the North.

Much of the worst of the eurozone debt crisis was stimulated by credit-financed wage and public spending increases over the last decade. The euro brought the nations of southern Europe low interest rates and easy credit: and they borrowed to finance increased public spending, government wages, and real estate programmes. Both the wage increases of the construction workers and the government employees were largely credit financed. Low interest rates in southern Europe meant that these countries could borrow very easily but failed to add to their productivity. Prices increased with this inflationary credit bubble, which had the knock-on effect of depriving these countries of their competitiveness. But the decline in profits was counterbalanced by the explosion of cheap credit in the euro's early years: a process which would itself lead to the credit crunch and worldwide recession. Until 2008, credit markets did not substantially reflect the economic differences between the countries of the eurozone. This resulted in a high co-movement in borrowing costs for these countries. This apparent 'convergence' of eurozone nations, however, reversed itself from 2008 onwards.

The competitiveness issue was exacerbated 10 years ago when Eastern European countries, with significantly lower wages, were absorbed into the EU. For comparison, Poland has wage costs of about €7 per hour – less than a third of (now unemployment-wracked) Spain, where they are at €23. No dream of any politician in Europe can overcome this fundamental problem of having the wrong wages and prices. This is a fundamental long-term structural problem – as opposed to a purely cyclical one of boom-and-bust finances that can (potentially) be supressed or mitigated by tempering regulation and economic policy.

The apparent success of the euro relied on tight monetary policy – so lack of budgetary control was bound to bring problems. Keeping stability in prices was a key principle for the European Central Bank (ECB) to control inflation. But as economic historian Robert Pringle pointed out in reference to the euro: 'It could not deal with the wider implications of the global financial system relating to International exchange rates and the impact of the fluctuating exchange with the weak dollar which ultimately made the euro uncompetitive in the world markets for its members especially for key export industries and tourism.'[2] Germany had kept a tight grip on wages. Its GDP is driven by its massive export market representing nearly 50% of GDP so remaining competitive was vital to its export industries. Indeed, Germany is so competitive *for the same reason* that southern Europe is now uncompetitive – because, in the credit inflation of the 2000s, they increased their prices relative to Germany.

Germany has been the main beneficiary of the euro prospering at the expense of its southern eurozone neighbours. It is because of exceptionally low interest rates that Greeks, Spaniards and Cypriots have bought German goods and cars, fuelling a massive credit boom in their countries. Before 1990, Germans moaned about the loss of the almighty Deutschmark, but stopped complaining when cheap credit skyrocketed its exports to these countries – its eurozone neighbours – that now are paying the price for profligacy.

By contrast, the South did not follow Germany's example and allowed wage inflation to rise and coupled this with a spending boom largely centred on the commercial and retail property markets (Spain, Portugal, Cyprus and Greece). With the global recession, these countries found the level of debt they had acquired unsustainable – with an equally unmanageable rise in borrowing costs. If these countries had not been straitjacketed by the single currency they could have devalued to become more competitive with their northern neighbours. Instead they faced austerity through the bailout provisions *and* internal devaluations causing cuts in wages, benefits and overall living standards. Greece provides the best illustration of how devastatingly the level of spending and salary cuts has affected the everyday lives of its citizens.

By contrast, while the eurozone giant's post-crisis recovery has been touted as an example of an economy of a country that made the short-term sacrifices necessary for long-term success, Germany did not apply to its economy the harsh, pro-cyclical austerity measures that are imposed on countries like Greece – even as it has benefitted from the low interest rates facilitated its thriving export markets in manufactured goods. A Bloomberg editorial entitled cast the role and responsibility of Germany in the debt crisis in this light:

> In the millions of words written about Europe's debt crisis, Germany is typically cast as the responsible adult and Greece as the profligate child. Prudent Germany, the narrative goes, is loath to bail out freeloading Greece, which borrowed more than it could afford and now must suffer the consequences... By December 2009, according to the Bank for International Settlements, German banks had amassed claims of $704 billion on Greece, Ireland, Italy, Portugal and Spain, much more than the German banks' aggregate net capital. In other words, they lent more than they could afford... Irresponsible borrowers can't exist without irresponsible lenders. Germany's banks were Greece's enablers.

It concluded, therefore, that 'Europe's taxpayers have provided as much financial support to Germany as they have to Greece.'[3]

Nor does the oft-touted stereotype of a lack of work ethic hold much weight. There have been widespread accusations that Greeks are not industrious but this perception is unreasonable and misleading. OECD data shows that the average Greek worker puts in one and a half times more hours per year than their typical German counterpart, and the average retirement age of a Greek is, at 61.7 years, older than that of a German.[4] Figures from the OECD show that the average Greek worker toils away for 2,017 hours per year, and those in Spain, Italy, and Portugal worked around the OECD average of 1,765. Out of the 34 members of the OECD, that is just two places behind the board leaders, South Korea. On the other hand, the average German worker – normally thought of as the embodiment of industriousness – manages 1,408 hours a year. That is just 33rd out of 34 on the OECD list, slightly above the Dutch (or 24th out of 25 looking at the European countries alone). Only one other OECD country's workers put in fewer hours, and that's the Netherlands with 1,377 hours. The average Greek is therefore working a full 40% longer than the average German.

There is a degree here to which very old and unpleasant stereotypes are being unearthed. Throughout history, Greeks have been liable to being portrayed as hedonistic, immoral and sinful: by Romans such as Cato the Elder, by Catholic theologians in the Middle Ages, and by generations of European scholarship since the Enlightenment, which accused them of contributing to the apparent degeneracies of Imperial Rome and the Byzantine Empire.[5]

The contrast between the condition of North and South cannot be attributed to the virtue of one half of the eurozone, versus the recklessness and lax spirit of the other. Instead, it illuminates the key weaknesses at the heart of an austerity-driven scheme for recovery. The whole point of the structural reforms enforced under the terms of the Troika is to make these troubled, debt-ridden eurozone economies more lean and competitive. But what makes an economy competitive in an international marketplace? Ultimately and finally, it is prices for a product or service which are not higher than elsewhere. The southern countries of the EU inflated under the credit bubble that the euro brought them. Undoing this inflation is a very different matter. Cutting nominal wages in a safe manner is extraordinarily difficult: as the example of Greece proves, it puts armies of protestors in the streets, destroys confidence, and shatters the social cohesion necessary to maintain a functioning socio-economic order.

Conversely, the very existence of the euro makes currency devaluation impossible. This removes the natural economic value for correcting these competitive variations. In these circumstances, the only thing austerity is good at contracting is economic output, which has a devastating effect on a nation's ability to both function as an economy, and pay the very debts such cuts are meant to facilitate. The realignment of relative prices that Greece and perhaps other countries need cannot really be achieved within the euro, because it would either mean astronomical inflation in the core or deflation in southern Europe. According to the economics department of Goldman Sachs, a German inflation of 70% would be needed to make southern Europe competitive without price cuts there. That is 5.5% annual inflation for ten years in Germany or an average inflation of 3.6% for the eurozone. Such numbers are now so extreme that they would wreak much of the same havoc as austerity has. Nor are they remotely compatible with the mandate of the ECB. It may be that a true recovery in the eurozone requires an eventual realignment of relative prices – meaning inflation in Germany, or deflation in southern Europe. Yet the entire region is now faced with deflation as a universal and homogenous economic threat.

Only a small number of people support an austerity-exclusive policy, but they are very influential and powerful. It has some limited support from the world of finance and big business, but is primarily endorsed by the big institutions of the eurozone: the IMF, the European Central Bank and (predominantly) the German elements of the European Union Commission, together with almost all the governments and major opposition parties of Europe (the latter, admittedly, to varying degrees). By contrast, austerity is conceived by the majority as trying to destroy people's living standards now and in the future. The disconnect between political class and popular consensus is a fissure at the heart of the entire European project – a godsend both to right-wing attacks on the creditability of the European Union itself, and leftist critiques of the political and financial infrastructure of European society.

The main purpose of the terms attached to the eurozone bailouts was to restore profitability after the global recession. Put simply, the idea at their heart has always been that too many eurozone nations have lived beyond their means for too long and now need to take responsibility for their profligacy. Budget retrenchment will ensure that countries live within their means while deregulation and privatisation of 'bloated' public services will make them leaner, fitter and more competitive economies.

If we were to answer the question of whether austerity works – or at least, in the way it was imposed in the bailout provisions for Greece and the eurozone, not necessarily as a universal abstraction – then the simple answer has to be 'no'.[6] As a result of these policies Greek unemployment stands at over 25% with youth unemployment closer to 40%, wages, welfare benefits and in turn living standards have plummeted by up to 50% and public debt increasing to 160% of GDP. It stood at 120% before the first austerity programme of 2010. Worse still, it is expected to rise further to 192% by the end of 2014.

The IMF–EU austerity measures have effectively seen Greece reduced from a developed to an underdeveloped country. Sources from the Greek side close to senior officials in Brussels, who wished to remain anonymous, suggests in strong, somewhat robust language that 'the middle class are being pauperised and destroyed,'[7] and that, despite an awareness of their own economic mismanagements, they feel 'a sense of betrayal by their European partners'. They further add that 'all the evidence points to the fact that the consequences of the austerity measures on its citizens is to promote social unrest on a worrying scale, and has promoted the growth of extremism as seen in the European election in May 2014.' Such opinions find plenty of corroboration in the data.

Underpinning the rationale of these policies has been the notion that Greece – as well as Ireland, Spain and Portugal – can recover by means of an internal pricing devaluation to replace the currency devaluation that a single currency straitjackets away as an option. This means increasing unemployment so much that wages fall enough to make the country more internationally competitive. The social costs of such a move, however, are extremely high, and the evidence it works thin. Unemployment has doubled in Greece (to 14.7%), more than doubled in Spain (to 20.7%) and more than tripled in Ireland (to 14.7%). But recovery is still elusive. The biggest problem facing a government in an austerity-driven economic spiral is how it can service debt repayments from an ever-dwindling source of revenue instead of investing in infrastructure and economic development. Of the 160 billion euros in new loans, in addition to the previous 160 billion euros, roughly 80% goes back to creditors to service past debts, 15% for Greek banks and 5% to pay existing government obligations to domestic and foreign creditors. Not a single euro of those 320 billion in bailout funds has gone towards economic development or social programmes. Small businesses (SMEs), the main drivers of a modern economy, are closing down at rate of 5,000 per month, not to mention the other 100,000 which have gone bankrupt since 2008. Those SME businesses that are actually able to trade and do business cannot grow as interest rates on loans are so prohibitively high in Greece and the Mediterranean, in contrast to what are effectively 'negative' interest rates in Germany: a scenario in which German banks are in effect paying the debtor to borrow. These circumstances are ironic, considering the EU's treasured ambition to enable the private sector to regenerate employment in Europe.

Whether in fact it would have been easier for the country to exit the single currency – aside from the constitutional crisis in the eurozone, and likely contagion effect – and undergo monetary devaluation is an important question to ask when looking at the calamitous effect of a single currency on the southern states of post-financial crisis Europe. EU ministers warned of a sharp increase in Greek debt from such devaluation if it were to have left the eurozone.[8] But the fact is that Greece would not pay this debt, as Argentina did not pay two-thirds of its foreign debt after its devaluation and default in 2002. Indeed, the main reason for Argentina's rapid recovery was that it was finally freed from adhering to fiscal and monetary policies that stifled growth. How can distressed economies that are frozen out of capital markets recover? By currency devaluation – or default, in the worst cases. For more than three and a half years Argentina had suffered through one of the deepest recessions of the 20th century. The Argentines took loans from the IMF and cut spending as poverty and unemployment soared. Then Argentina defaulted on its foreign debt and cut loose from the dollar. Most economists and the business press predicted that years of disaster would ensue. But the economy shrank for just one more quarter after the devaluation and default; it then grew 63% over the next six years, and received a substantial boost from the devaluation's effect on the trade balance, making its exports far more competitive.[9] Of course, the infrastructure of the single currency renders these options impossible for member states such as Greece.

From a creditors' point of view – the view which European Union authorities have apparently adopted – a country that has accumulated too much debt must be punished, so as not to encourage 'bad behaviour'. A chief Merkel economic advisor went as far as to say that emergency bailouts to Greece and future EU aid recipients should bring with it harsh penalties. But punishing an entire country for the past mistakes of some of its leaders, while morally satisfying to some, is hardly the basis for sound policy. Indeed, it is worth noting in this respect the special irony that France and Germany were among the first countries to break the Stability and Growth Pact – an agreement which forbids member states to have more than 3% of budget deficit to GDP, while Spain and Ireland ran surpluses before the 2008 crisis. Germany was in breach of the deficit/debt rule in 1998–99, 2002–05 and 2008–10. Such a fact sits ill at ease with the unyielding rhetoric from the two countries about the indulgent and dissolute behaviour of a profligate South.

In March 2013, Cyprus did not have a sympathetic audience. It had long delayed its plea for assistance, and that was used as an excuse to bear down heavily on its request for help. It was easy to present the island as its own villain, a victim of its own hubris, with the lure of casino banking and corrupt Russian money proving its undoing. Such a message could be tuned to the mood of an embittered German public. The final bail-in/bailout package was sold as punishing oligarchs to protect the ordinary public, but the economic implications of the bail-in conditions still hit those many Cypriots – or foreign nationals without a Smaug-sized savings balance, but who held accounts in the same banks as the rich Russian, Ukrainian and other non-EU depositors. The criticisms vented at the economic infrastructure of the nation had been curiously absent during the boom years. Before the global downturn in 2008, the IMF had described Cyprus's economic performance as a 'long period of high growth, low unemployment, and sound public finances'. The effect of the Greek PSI deal of November 2011 on the two main banks, coupled with the AKEL Government's spending spree between 2008 and 2013 soon changed that analysis. It does go to show that without those two critical factors, a rescue may have been avoided or limited to dealing with the banks' bad loan portfolio and restructuring the public sector – an exercise recommended and conducted in even the more healthy economies of the eurozone.

While many important figures in the EU have attempted to down-play the structural significance of the Cyprus crisis, it quickly proved key to the case for a unified Banking Union Directive. The European Commission made this extremely clear in a statement for 'A Single Resolution Mechanism for the Banking Union' on the July 10, 2013, two months after the bail-in:

> The recent financial crisis in Cyprus highlighted the need for swift and decisive action backed by EU-level funding arrangements in order to avoid a situation in which bank resolution conducted at national level would have a disproportionate impact on the real economy, and to curb uncertainty and prevent bank runs and contagion of other parts of the euro area and the Single Market.

The plan for this scheme was therefore outlined according to these lessons:

> The proposed Directive on Bank Recovery and Resolution (BRRD) would, when adopted, determine the rules for how EU banks in difficulties were restructured, how vital functions for the real econ-omy were maintained, and how losses and costs were allocated to the banks' shareholders and creditors. It would provide more com-prehensive and effective arrangements to deal with failing banks at national level, as well as arrangements to tackle cross-border banking failures.[10]

The issue of the nexus between bank and sovereign debt is essential to the financial health of the eurozone. Exposure levels saw only the most minimal cuts in 2013, and continue to climb. Consequently, they remain extremely vulnerable to another sovereign debt crisis. There is a continuing need for the eurozone to split off bank from sovereign debt and decouple this toxically close relationship between private and state finances. This resolution is therefore an attempt to actually get to grips with this problem.

Federalism is essential to the purpose and function of such a Banking Directive. This scheme would only be available to those eurozone members that sign up to the Single Supervisory Mechanism

(SSM). Secondly, it will help to cut the link between bank debt and sovereign debt – a bond central to the collapse of state finances in the eurozone – and help to protect depositor holders from the effect of bail-ins as happened in the Cyprus crisis. To benefit from the scheme, eurozone banks participating in the scheme will have to make contributions to the European Resolution Fund (ERF). The impact of this – the financing of the ERF by contributions from participating banks – would make resolution funding more efficient for the banks concerned.

Most importantly, the Economic and Financial Affairs Council of the European Union stated in a press release on February 19, 2014, that 'bail-in and not bailout is the main guiding principle for bank resolution'.[11] If any clearer evidence is needed that the rescue plan tested in Cyprus has been made a cornerstone of future EU policy, it is contained in those words.

While Cyprus gets to grips with its recovery, attention has turned to the rest of the eurozone, as the message being voiced loud and clear is that other larger economies in the club are still behind on privatisation and overdue structural reforms. Statements such as 'the currency union faces another "lost decade"' voiced by Hans-Werner Sinn, president of the Munich based IFO Institute, seem dramatic but convey a generally held feeling that not much is working for the euro at present resulting in continued stagnation and low growth.[12] For Sinn, the political implication of this 'growing animosity towards the European project', just when he believes that 'Europe...has no alternative but to unite'.[13]

Although the euro was supposed to draw EU members closer together it has in fact pulled them apart: *politically* as well as economically. The pursuit of austerity has not helped solve the structural weakness of competitively disparate economies locked in the straitjacket of a single currency. The acute phase of the financial crisis, where Greece was in imminent and immediate danger of default, may have subsided, but it is being replaced with a political battle for Europe's future direction: a phase in which the Cyprus deal represents the shots. 'The acute phase of the financial crisis is now over,' said the US financier George Soros, 'Future crises will be political in origin.' He foresaw a bleak period of Japanese-style stagnation worsened by constant bickering between EU national leaders. 'What was meant to be a voluntary association of equal states has now been transformed by the euro crisis into a relationship between creditor and debtor countries that is neither voluntary nor equal. Indeed, the euro could destroy the EU altogether.'[14] Fear of the impact of a more extremist brand of politics helps to explain the current aversion in much of Europe to the crisis solutions scripted in Berlin. Merkel herself used the centenary of the Great War to liken the situation to that of 1914: complaining of complacency amongst the political old guard and warning of the sleepwalking European leaders who led the continent into the First World War.

## Monetary Union: Stability or Systemic Weakness?

The dream of the architects of European monetary union was the creation of an 'island of stability' in an economically and financially turbulent world. Such claims were repeated, apparently without irony, by ECB President Mario Draghi at a press conference in Frankfurt in March 2014, when he discussed the historically low and almost deflationary interest rates for the region.[15] Whatever the debateable achievements or blunders of the single currency experiment, it is undeniable that the existence of a single currency, without the corresponding fiscal integration or political union normally underpinning a sole monetary standard, has introduced massive new sources of strain to the region, while doing nothing to shield it from macroeconomic disturbances abroad. It has given the European arena of the global crisis its own particular flavour of financial trouble. Countries crippled by the burden of sovereign debt, such as Greece, have not been able to devalue their currency to reduce the load. Indeed, surges at strength in the euro at critical junctures, most notably 2009 and late 2010, have wreaked havoc on their ability to service their debt, triggering repeated fears of impending default.

At the heart of the financial infrastructure of the eurozone lies the European Central Bank. The principal task of the ECB is to keep inflation under control. The institution's scope of monetary policy is defined almost exclusively as 'maintaining an environment of stable prices'.[16] It has as its central philosophy a pure and orthodox form of Freidman's monetarism. The euro is the only major monetary construction in the world whose central bank explicitly erased the objective of employment from monetary policy, based on monetarist recommendations. Erasing the external accounts imbalances as the main issue at stake in the monetary construction is, arguably, the most extraordinary feature of the single currency making. It means that policy makers are concerned simply with the public, rather than private, side of external accounts.

Consequently, ECB has always shunned the kind of quantitative easing so eagerly employed by the US Federal Reserve. And yet, to save the eurozone from dissolution, the ECB has adopted measures that far exceed its original mandate, and are beyond any previous conception of its proper role. To help bolster the eurozone's economy, Mario Draghi has kept interest rates low and used cheap-rate long-term loans to pump liquidity into European lenders, promising to do 'whatever it takes' to save the currency bloc. The ECB is widely expected to start its own QE programme to try to combat potential deflation and jolt sagging growth in the eurozone (ironically, just as the Federal Reserve in the US ends its own). This has contributed to the fact that the euro's value against the dollar has been sinking to levels last seen two years ago. If the ECB does act, downward pressure on Europe's common currency will intensify – though it would result in exports becoming more competitive, a boon at least for the German economy.

The other major institution of the Troika, the IMF, has also gone a long way to change its tune on the economic path for Europe. Faced with low growth in the global economy, and especially the eurozone, the IMF has urged governments to start spending again to buoy growth. This supreme *volte-face* comes as the evidence piles up that austerity – at least in IMF and Troika-espoused formulation – has run into the ground as a strategy for dealing with debt. 'The global economy faces the prospect of prolonged subpar growth, accompanied by high unemployment and rising inequality,' Christine Lagarde said ahead of the autumn 2014 meetings of the IMF and the World Bank. While she still stressed the need for fiscal discipline, Lagarde strongly suggested a shift in the IMF's focus towards investment and spending to boost economies across the globe. Therefore, Lagarde argues, 'a much higher premium needs to be put across the membership on policies aimed at decisively raising today's actual and tomorrow's potential growth.' In particular, this includes 'more growth-friendly fiscal policies' that would 'support job market reforms'.[17] The IMF may technically be the subordinate partner in the Troika, but it is the one that has been calling the shots for the Greek economy these past four years, and it is the one in charge of putting numbers on the page. It repeatedly projected economic recoveries for 2011, 2012, and 2013 that did not materialise. The IMF estimates at least a 20% decline in wages and salaries for 2010–2014; but this has not been enough to make Greek exports significantly more competitive, according to the Fund's July 2013 review.[18] Exports have remained weak and haven't come close to compensating for the fiscal tightening and reduced domestic private spending. The strategy of 'internal devaluation' has not yet worked for Greece, nor – according to the IMF's data and analysis – for the eurozone as whole.[19]

After six years of effective economic depression, Greece has returned to growth in the third quarter of 2014, as promised by the IMF a year earlier.[20] The explanation for this is hard to attribute to traditional austerity programmes, however. For one thing, Greece may have benefitted from a mild amount of relative deflation. Greece in 2013 had the lowest inflation rate of the eurozone, with prices falling by 0.9%. Consumer price inflation turned negative for the first time since 1968. This has been good news both for disposable income and competitiveness.

But the most substantial factor may well be stimulus spending. In December 2013, the Greek parliament approved a substantial programme involving highway construction –according to the Ministry of Infrastructure, Transport, and Networks, total spending on this project will be €7.5 billion for 2014–15, or almost 3% of GDP. This stimulus likely made the difference between thin growth and another year of recession. Furthermore, most of the financing comes from European Union grants, so it does not add to Greece's debt. Ironically, German Finance Minister Wolfgang Schäuble, one of the fiercest defenders of fiscal discipline in Europe, has reacted to these changes by saying it would be 'foolish' to deviate from the eurozone's current focus on reducing member states' budget deficits – and that there was little point to state investment in infrastructure.

Increasingly the evidence suggests that the debt and financial problems of Europe may necessitate, or at least provoke, the kind of radical moves seen in Cyprus. The German economy, the locomotive of the great European project – and the bailout schemes for its salvation – is running out of steam. German growth is faltering, with the IMF cutting its growth outlook to 1.4% for 2014 and 1.5% in 2015. This is still better than the anaemic eurozone average, but well below peers like the UK, where the economy is expected to expand by 3.2% in 2014, and 2.7% the year after, and the United States. Yields on 10-year German Bunds plummeted to an all-time low in October 2014 as their flight-to-safety value rose to reach levels never seen before in any major European country in recorded history. Core inflation is barely above 0.2% for the eurozone at the time of writing.[21] The markets fear that deflation is becoming serious enough to threaten the fragile debt dynamics of weaker eurozone states. These yields are pricing in not just a continued slump, but default and exit risks. Simultaneously to this, the South is experiencing a huge contraction in bank credit.

# Conclusion

Eurozone leaders are finding it more difficult with each bailout rescue to balance their economic decisions with the political implications they create. In spite of its small size, Cyprus has been no exception to this trend – despite being sold as something different, unique, and irrelevant to the wider scheme of things. Brussels demanded that the bailout for Cypriot banks be partly paid for by the deposits of those banks – to the tune of €7 billion of the €17 billion the rescue package required. That demand essentially violated the social contract upon which the sanctity of bank deposits is founded. Since the Great Depression, advanced industrial nations had operated on the fundamental principle that deposits in banks were utterly secure – the money did not truly belong to the bank, who held it on behalf of the depositor as a trustee. Deposits were regarded as the one truly riskless placements of money – guaranteed by the insurance policies of the bank, and at last resort by the state. They were not regarded as investment bonds paying fixed amounts of interest, whose value would disappear if the bank failed. The only threat to their value was inflation.

The economic and political consequence of the Cyprus crisis is that the European Union has now made it official policy, under certain circumstances, to demand that member states seize depositors' assets to pay for the rescue of their financial institutions. If you are a business, a saver, retiree, investor, or anyone else with cause to have a moderately large deposit account, then the safety of your money depends, at the last resort, on the political considerations of the European Union and the IMF. A practice that used to offer high liquidity, no risk, and minimal returns, now offers conditional liquidity, minimal returns, and risks which are absolutely unknown.

The insecurity that these measures produced made it absolutely essential for Brussels to promote the potentially 'criminal', and certainly immoral, nature of Russian deposits. It was an easy story to sell to the European media, and one many former members or allies of AKEL in Cyprus – eager to wash their own hands of any culpability for a bankrupt state – could jump on board with. The narrative of casino banking and 'criminal' Russians makes the Cyprus case sound exceptional and unique – a tiny island which attracted illicit wealth, and got burned by its own greed in the process.

The Troika has established a new option for dealing with deposits in troubled banks. That principle would now seem to apply to all of Europe, most especially the eurozone. How and when it could be invoked is not easy to say: but those countries with money centres facing potentially similar problems to Cyprus would most likely be first in line. In both Malta and Luxemburg, the financial system outstrips GDP by similar margins to that of Cyprus at the time of the crisis, albeit their domestic banks represent a lower proportion of the total exposure of the sector.

Moreover, the precedent set has far wider ramifications than for other pocket financial centres. The point of a global banking system is that money is safe wherever it is deposited. Once that principle is revoked, anything is possible when given the right political and financial conditions. If Russian money can be seized from banks in Nicosia, what about Chinese deposits in Luxemburg, or American money in Malta? This is to say nothing of the fact that targeting specific groups still leaves a broad swathe of collateral victims. Cypriots and non-Russians lost, sometimes substantial, sums in the deposit seizure: and many of those who did were far less personally able to endure the cost than the super-wealthy 'oligarchs' Brussels claimed were being punished.

We must ask ourselves, finally, about why the Troika would have created this extraordinarily risky precedent. One answer is that they were genuinely confident that they could convince depositors – rightly or wrongly – that Cyprus was genuinely one of a kind. Certainly, the story that was sold to the press and people of Europe was simple and clear. Nor was it wholly unsuccessful, as many bought into this narrative.

The other answer was that they had no choice. Germany in early 2013 was hamstrung by the demands of the election cycle and the mood of an embittered public. A smaller bailout, with punitive strings attached, may have made the perfect electoral package. But this explanation is just the tip of the iceberg. The banking system of the recession-ridden eurozone is quite likely too big to salvage in the event of a serious crisis. Greece itself, only a small fraction of its GDP, required effectively a structured default – couched in the terms of a 'PSI' scheme – on its bond obligations to be rescued from insolvency. Any solution to a larger financial crisis may involve the loss of depositor's funds. But openly contemplating such an approach could itself lead to a run on the banks. If depositors decided that more 'bail-ins' were looming, then businesses and corporations round the globe could start pulling their cash out of European banks and parking it elsewhere. Those withdrawals could create a massive liquidity crisis in Europe. In light of this paradox, the Cypriot crisis offers the perfect compromise – an opportunity to test the principle of an enforced bail-in, whilst simultaneously offering plausible grounds for denying it had any wider implication. Cyprus therefore has the advantage of setting a precedent while not *appearing* to be a precedent at the same time.

It cannot be clear precisely what the EU and IMF negotiators were thinking in drafting this policy. Nevertheless, the first and simplest explanation for the terms offered was severely undermined on March 25, 2013, when Eurogroup President Jeroen Dijsselbloem said that Cyprus could serve as a template for future EU bailouts. Although he was quick to rescind the statement, the retraction does not exactly restore confidence this was not on their minds. The Council of the European Union has amplified the impression that a bail-in is part of the new infrastructure of any future rescue plans. And what is not a matter of debate is that the ruling institutions of the eurozone have broken a barrier that has been in place since the bank failures on the 1930s – and then went to enormous lengths to make excuses for it. Whatever the precedent proves in practical terms, the uncertainty this move generates is very real. In Europe, depositing money in a bank is no longer a move without risk.

There is a political as well as purely economic dimension to these trends which needs to be considered. Since the rise to prominence of the issue of the European debt crisis from 2009, commentators across the political spectrum have predicted the imminent collapse of the single currency; or at the very least the break-up of part of the eurozone. So far this has not yet come to pass. But the toll of repeated bailouts and austerity measures has been exceptionally high. The European project, launched in the wake of the devastation of the Second World War, faces not just an economic but an existential crisis as the political and popular will for such a dream totters under the weight of social and fiscal realities.

This is not entirely the result of the financial crisis. The dream of European integration has been struck by other headwinds in the recent past – most notably in 2005, when French and Dutch voters rejected a proposed Constitution of Europe by a wide margin.

But this time, the entire establishment has been indicted in a wave of support for populist and dissident movements from across the political spectrum. In the European elections of May 2014, the nationalist and (in most respects) hardline conservative UKIP and the National Front each won about a quarter of the vote in their home nations of Britain and France – with UKIP being the first outsider party to win seats in a British national election in over 100 years – and more extreme parties flourished in Sweden, Denmark, Austria and Hungary. Such groups are drawn from the more radical poles of both the Left and Right. The French National Front, Dutch Freedom Party and Danish People's Party articulate the causes of economic stress according to a different set of values to SYRIZA in Greece, or the Dutch Socialists. The only common denominator for these groups is dissent towards the entire European project – the source of their rising tide of support. In terms of the old left–right divide, European politics appears its most polarised since the Cold War – save for a convergence on this single, central issue.

The ongoing crisis, of which Cyprus is the latest and most novel manifestation, exposes a deep contradiction at the heart of Europe – between the Eurozone's need for successful integration, and voters' (and protestors') overwhelming rejection of it. If such populism continues to rise, it would not be a large leap from here for a member of the single currency to win a democratic mandate to quit it altogether – a Lehman-like event which would not only reignite the worst of the crisis, but put the survival of the entire project in the balance. Political upsets can be much harder to put to rights than economic ones, and it would not take much to bring a party like SYRIZA to power, or at least hold the balance of power – as was feared in the snap presidential election in Greece in December 2014, which sent markets tumbling.[1]

The possibility of such populism being satiated by a return to economic growth appears dubious. Unemployment levels in the EU remain extreme, at around 24–25 million people at the end of 2014 – three quarters of whom are in the eurozone.[2] Debt remains dangerously high, and with the region teetering on the edge of deflation, could rapidly worsen. The region may well be trapped in a 'lost decade' similar to that of Japan in the 1990s. But politically, the EU would be far less likely to survive such an experience intact than Japan: a nation state which had centuries to form a cohesive identity.

Ultimately this is an issue where democracy converges somewhat destructively with economics. The battle to save the euro has led to the unprecedented centralisation of authority in the EU over banking, taxes, budgets and welfare. It has produced the steady accretion of powers to the ECB, the European Commission and the European Parliament. Bailout terms have been dictated from the top, and voters in stricken countries have largely lost the ability to define the policy of their own governments. This transfer of powers is the result of economic failure, not success, and enforced without the endorsement of the public. The chances of it being accepted or tolerated are slim. Resentment and hostility towards Brussels, the eurozone, and the EU itself will continue to rise. Such sentiments are as strong in France now as in famously Eurosceptic Britain, or the austerity-afflicted PIGS.

Such a change in approach has been reflected in the victory of the young, leftist and anti-establishment SYRIZA party in Greece. The new Greek government won its mandate on the promise of ending the austerity measures imposed by the Troika – namely that they would 'tear up' the bailout memorandum.

Even those demanding adherence to the bailout agreement have recognised that has involved the most punishing recession seen anywhere in the developed world. Moreover, Greece's debts have reached the point at which it has become all but impossible to actually pay them. Nevertheless, a mandate from its electorate does not mean the government will be able to dictate the terms of their country's bailout. Within a month, the government was accused of backtracking on its election promises over the four-month extension to the bailout terms agreed by the former 'Troika' – in a tidy act of rebranding, it is now referred to simply as the 'institutions' of the EU, and the 'memorandum of understanding' has become the 'agreement'. How these negotiations will resolve themselves, and how far SYRIZA will back down, are unclear. But Greece's debt, at 175% of GDP, is going nowhere, and the threat of default and an exit from the single currency may well hang over Greece until it actually happens.

Although little seems to have immediately changed in the method of bailout enforcement as the 'Troika' members continue to remain the monitors of the programme, SYRIZA has done much to challenge the approach taken so far, and put back into serious political discourse the possibility of alternative proposals for meeting its debt obligations that do not so dramatically stifle the ability of the economy to grow.

Outside Greece itself, the recent direction for the eurozone appears to have been one towards greater consensus and calm. The ECB was widely expected to begin a quantitative easing programme in Q1 2015, at the very latest. Consequently, 2014 saw a significant rally in sovereign-bond markets throughout the troubled economies of the Mediterranean. The yield on the Spanish 10-year bond hit 2.1% from a high of 7% – those of Portugal fell from 6.2% to 2.7%. What was perhaps less expected, however, was the sheer size of the final programme – €60 billion a month – and its open-ended timeframe, scheduled as it is to run at least until September 2016, and until a 2% inflation target is reached.

By adopting the euro, the old option of devaluation did not exist for countries plagued with sovereign debt. The downward pressure that QE will likely exert on the currency – as evidenced in the steady decline of the dollar during the three Federal Reserve QE programmes – may be at least a partial ameliorant to that. A fall in the euro will also push up import prices which will add something to inflation on its own. Nevertheless, the implementation of these programmes in Britain, America and Japan has not removed the threat of deflation, with inflation falling to just 0.3% in the UK in January 2015 – and that is without considering the additional structural pressures and demand problems of the eurozone. The need for the ECB to so radically alter the direction of its monetary policy is clear, but not its likelihood of sustained success.

While Cyprus saw its own wave of (remarkably peaceful) popular protests to the Troika deal in the latter days of March, 2013, there has been little in the way of a new injection of radicalism in the nation's politics. A big part of this is likely the fact that the primary embodiment of the Far Left, AKEL, is part of the nation's establishment itself – and held office for five years immediately preceding the bailout. Furthermore, the island's relatively strong and robust recovery is a marked contrast to its other Mediterranean peers, especially Greece. Its recession has only been a fraction of the relative size. The danger of this, of course, is that it provides a massive spur to the (misleading) argument that the bail-in is the basis of that recovery,[3] and so enhances its value as a precedent, and emboldens the Troika to do the same. Cyprus is the fifth nation in the eurozone to be bailed out, and the first where the burden was shifted onto depositors. With the deteriorating finances of the eurozone, the threat of deflation, and the loss of political will for traditional austerity packages, it is unlikely to be the last.

# Notes

## 1 Birth of a Nation

1. This list includes: the UN Secretary-General's legal adviser, high-level UNFICYP military personnel and also the UN Under-Secretary General for Special Political Affairs. This earlier research providing background to political and security issues is combined with more recent (transcripted) interviews with officials in the banking, legal and political establishment closest to the events surrounding the bail-in negotiations of 2013–2013. See John Theodorides, 'Legal Aspects of United Nations Peace Keeping Operations with Special Reference to Cyprus and the Middle East 1964–1979' The subject of a LLM Thesis in Public International Law The University of Manchester, December 1979.
2. EOKA is an acronym of *Ethniki Organosis Kyprion Agoniston*, or the 'National Organisation of Cypriot Fighters'.
3. Kyriacos Markides, 'Social Change and the Rise and Decline of Social Movements: The Case of Cyprus', American Ethnologist, I (1974), pp. 309–330.
4. Treaty of Establishment 16th August 1960. See http://www.mfa.gr/images/docs/kypriako/treaty_of_establishment.pdf
5. For more background see http://www.securitycouncilreport.org/special-research-report/lookup-c-glKWLeMTIsG-b-4474149.php?print=true
6. http://www.mfa.gov.tr/page-3-the-law.en.mfa
7. UN Charter Article 1(2)
8. See Polyvious Polyviou, *Cyprus: Conflict and Negotiation, 1960–1980*, London: Holmes & Meier Publishers Inc, 1981), p. 14ff.
9. http://www.cyprus-conflict.net/Moran%20-%20UN%2064%20-%20pt2.html
10. http://www.cyprus-conflict.net/Moran%20-%20UN%2064%20-%20pt2.html
11. Paragraph 129 of the Report of the Secretary General, March 1965.
12. S. A. De Smith, *The New Commonwealth and its Constitutions* (London: Steven and Sons, 1964), p. 285.
13. Op. cit., p. 296.
14. For more on this see http://www.cyprus-conflict.net/patrick%20chp%204%20pt%202.html
15. The fighting in Nicosia during December 1963 is outlined in the 21–31 December issues of the Cyprus Mall, Cyprus Bulletin, and the Special News Bulletin. Secondary sources include: Stephens, 1966, pp. 181–185; C. Foley, 1964, pp. 168–171.
16. http://www.cyprus-conflict.net/Ball%20-%2064.html
17. Joseph S. Joseph, 'Cyprus: Ethnic Conflict and International Politics', (London: St Martin's Press, 1997), p. 66.

18. The General Assembly adopted on 18 December 1965 Resolution 2077 (XX), for which see http://www.hri.org/Cyprus/Cyprus_Problem/UNdocs/gad2077.html
19. UNFICYP was established by Security Council Resolution 186 (1964)
20. Galo Plaza report 1965 para. 72, http://www.cyprus-conflict.net/galo%20plaza%20-%20pt%203.html
21. Galo Plaza report 1965 para. 73, http://www.cyprus-conflict.net/galo%20plaza%20-%20pt%203.html
22. Galo Plaza report 1965 para. 153, http://www.cyprus-conflict.net/galo%20plaza%20-%20pt%203.html
23. Polyvios Polyviou, *Cyprus In Search of a Constitution: Constitutional Negotiations and Proposals, 1960–1975* (Nicosia, 1976).
24. Brendan O'Malley and Ian Craig, The Cyprus Conspiracy: America, Espionage and the Turkish Invasion (London: I. B. Tauris, 1999), offers a dissenting opinion in considerable detail.
25. http://www.timeshighereducation.co.uk/features/what-jim-knew-and-henry-did/148781.article
26. In July 1974 a low level shuttle diplomacy by Joseph Sisco, Undersecretary of State for Political Affairs to Athens and Ankara failed to do more than avert open warfare between Greece and Turkey and failed to halt the invasion.
27. Andrekos Varnava and Hubert Faustmann (eds.), *Reunifying Cyprus: The Annan Plan and Beyond (London: I.B. Tauris, 2001)* , p. 13.
28. Polyviou, p. 48.
29. http://www.cyprus-conflict.net/narrative-main-%203.html

## 2   Forever Divided?

1. William Mallison, *Cyprus: A Modern History* (London: I.B Tauris, 2005), p. 81.
2. Eric Solsten (ed.), *Cyprus: A Country Study* (Washington: GPO for the Library of Congress, 1991), pp. 35–37.
3. Alexandros Nafpliotis, *Britain and the Greek Colonels: Accommodating the Junta in the Cold War* (London: I.B. Tauris, 2012).
4. U.S. critics of the coup included then-Senator Lee Melcalf, who criticised the Johnson Administration for providing aid to a 'military regime of collaborators and Nazi sympathisers'.
5. Solsten, p. 32.
6. Andrew Borowiec, *The Mediterranean Feud* (New York: Praeger Publishers, 1983).
7. http://content.time.com/time/magazine/article/0,9171,911440,00.html
8. Christos Kassimeris, 'Greek Response to the Cyprus Invasion', *Small Wars and Insurgencies*, XIX (2008), pp. 256–273.
9. UN Resolution 186 (1964), extended and modified after the invasion under Resolution 383 (1975).
10. S/11900; S/11568; S/11717; S/11789/ S/12253 (UN Security Council Resolutions for 1975).

11. Transcript of interview held June 2ⁿᵈ 2014.
12. http://news.bbc.co.uk/onthisday/hi/dates/stories/july/20/newsid_3866 000/3866521.stm
13. Art 1V of the Treaty of Guarantee, 'In so far as common or concerted action may not prove possible, each of the three guaranteeing powers reserve the right to take action with the sole aim of re-establishing the state of affairs created by the present treaty.'
14. Even if unilateral was permitted under the Treaty, it would have been of a temporary nature to restore constitutional order. Concerted action by all three guaranteeing powers was the rightful way forward in exercising the terms of the treaty.
15. Specifically the North Atlantic Treaty, the foundational agreement of NATO, signed in Washington, D.C. on 4ᵗʰ April 1949.
16. The nearest Greek Airforce base in Crete was 400 miles from Cyprus giving it a distinct military disadvantage.
17. http://www.timeshighereducation.co.uk/features/what-jim-knew-and-henry-did/148781.article
18. In a letter to the editor published in *The Economist*, Feb 1975, the author argued that the Turkish Cypriots were the minority numerically but were the 'majority' in respect of fire power because of the Turkish army dominance.
19. http://www.timeshighereducation.co.uk/features/what-jim-knew-and-henry-did/148781.article
20. http://www.timeshighereducation.co.uk/features/what-jim-knew-and-henry-did/148781.article
21. AKEL only held power as part of a coalition until being elected to govern in its own right in 2008.
22. For which see Craig and O' Malley.
23. Henry Kissinger, *Years of Renewal: The Concluding Volume of His Memoirs* (New York: Simon & Schuster, 1999). See also Christopher Hitchens, *Hostage to History: Cyprus from the Ottomans to Kissinger* (London: Verso, 1997).
24. http://www.timeshighereducation.co.uk/features/what-jim-knew-and-henry-did/148781.article
25. Notable under the terms of the Treaty of Sevres, ratified in August 1920. For more on this see Paul C. Helmreich, *From Paris to Sèvres: The Partition of the Ottoman Empire at the Peace Conference of 1919–1920* (Columbus: Ohio State University Press, 1974).
26. Meltem Muftuler-Bac and Aylin Guney, 'The European Union and the Cyprus Problem, 1961–2003,' *Middle Eastern Studies*, XXI (2005), pp. 281–293, quote on p. 285.
27. Commission of the European Communities opinion on the Application by the Republic of Cyprus for Membership, Com (93) 313 Final. Published 30ᵗʰ June 1998.
28. Report of the UN Secretary-General on his mission of good offices in Cyprus, 28 May 2004(S/2004/437), Paragraph 61. Talat refers to the strong involvement of Greece and Turkey in the negotiations of core

security issues like the presence of Greek and Turkish troops, an international force or the Treaty of Guarantee.

29. Annex 1X, 'Coming into Being of the New State of Affairs', Article 6, p. 138 specifies the new steps in the relationship with the EU of the unified state, 'Upon entry into force of the Foundation Agreement, the Co-Presidents shall through the attached letter inform the European Union of the coming into being of the new state of affairs and the commitment of the United Cyprus Republic to assume all rights and obligations arising from the Treaty of Accession. The Co-Presidents shall also request the European Union to endorse the Foundation Agreement and to accommodate its terms in line with the principles on which the European Union is founded and adopt special measures for the Turkish Cypriot State. They shall furthermore request that the final outcomes will result in the adaptation of primary law and ensure legal certainty and security within the European Union legal system for all concerned.' Published online at http://www.hri.org/docs/annan/AnnexIX/AnnexIX.pdf

30. Op. cit., Article 1.1, p. 137.

31. Nathalie Tocci, 'Reflections on Post-referendum Cyprus', *The International Spectator: Italian Journal of International Affairs* (2008), published online at http://www.tandfonline.com/doi/pdf/10.1080/03932720408457082

32. Varnava, A., & Faustmann, B (Eds.) (2011) *Reunifying Cyprus: The Annan Plan and Beyond*. London: I.B. Tauris & Co. It should be noted here that the Turkish military had always been more involved than the diplomats in outlining the core demands of the Turkish side. This is not surprising as it reflects the influence held by the Turkish military on domestic politics although increasingly less so in recent years.

33. http://www.hri.org/docs/annan/AnnexIV/AnnexIV.pdf

34. Coughlan, R. 'From Corporate Autonomy to the Search for Territorial Federalism', in Guy, Y. (ed.), *Autonomy and Ethnicity: Negotiating Completing Claims in Multi-Ethnic States* (Cambridge: Cambridge University Press, 1999)

35. Mumtaz Soysal 'Mistakes and Deception', published in Turkish centre-left newspaper Cumhuriyet, 2nd April 2005.

36. This heralded a period (albeit a short-lived one) when the 'doves' in the TRNC were in the majority.

37. It would be 14 years before the reductions in Turkish troops was scaled down to 3000.

38. http://www.academia.edu/219002/Cyprus_Security_Concerns_and_the_Failure_of_the_Annan_Plan. The poll was conducted by the Greek Cypriot TV channel 'Mega'. Only 13% cited a desire to live separately as a primary goal. The other consideration offered was economic.

39. Tocci (2008).

40. For further reading see Christalla Yakinthou, *Political Settlements in Divided Societies: Consociationalism and Cyprus* (London: Palgrave Macmillian, 2009) throws light on the challenges of adopting political

settlements in frozen conflicts and divided societies by focusing on the conflict in Cyprus, arguing that elite intransigence has held back the possibility of a workable power-sharing solution coming to fruition.

41. As reported in the Guardian on the 22ⁿᵈ April 2004, http://www. theguardian.com/world/2004/apr/22/eu.cyprus
42. http://www.unannanplan.agrino.org/1revisedunplan.pdf
43. Rebecca Bryant, 'An Ironic Result in Cyprus', *Middle East Report Online* (2004), available at http://www.cyprus-conflict.net/Annan%20plan% 20rejected.html.
44. http://news.bbc.co.uk/1/hi/world/europe/3656653.stm
45. U.N. Secretary General, Press Conference, UN Headquarters, New York, 28 April 2004.
46. http://www.mfa.gov.tr/what-the-world-said-after-the-referanda.en.mfa
47. From the 'Presidency Conclusions' in the Council of the European Union, 12–13ᵗʰ December 2002, proceedings of which were published in Brussles, 29ᵗʰ January 2003.
48. From 'Cyprus: A Greek Wrecker', *The Economist*, April 15ᵗʰ 2004.
49. Varnava and Faustmann, p. 213.

# 3   The Financial Crisis Spreads to Cyprus

1. From a transcripted interview with the authors.
2. http://www.reuters.com/article/2013/03/22/us-cyprus-banks-idUSBRE92 L0CQ20130322, see also his profile at http://www2.parliament.cy/ parliamenteng/003_02_biography/papageorgiou_pampos.htm
3. http://www.bbc.com/news/business-21831943
4. PIMCO, 'Independent Due Diligence of the Banking System of Cyprus' (February 2013), pp. 8–9, published online at http://www.centralbank. gov.cy/media/pdf/CyprusIndependentDueDiligenceReport_18April.pdf
5. Op. cit., p. 9.
6. Op. cit., p. 8, http://www.centralbank.gov.cy/media/pdf/CyprusIndepen dentDueDiligenceReport_18April.pdf
7. Op. cit., pp. 10–11.
8. 'Memorandum of Understanding on Specific Economic Policy Conditionality', p. 2, http://static.cyprus.com/troika_memo_final.pdf
9. From a transcripted interview with the authors.
10. From the 'Concise Monetary Policy Report', the Central Bank of Cyprus, Economic Research Department, Published in February 2005.
11. Michael Sarris suggests that 'capital inflows, mainly from Russia' were 'helping to create the housing bubble'. From an interview with the authors on the 4ᵗʰ June, 2014.
12. http://articles.chicagotribune.com/2013-03-22/business/sns-rt-us-cyprus-banksbre92l0ly-20130322_1_euro-zone-central-bank-cypriot-banks
13. From an interview with the authors on the 4ᵗʰ June, 2014.
14. http://www.theglobaleconomy.com/Cyprus/Economic_growth/
15. http://www.bloomberg.com/news/2011-07-29/recession-took-bigger-bite-out-of-u-s-economy-than-previously-estimated.html

16. Petmesidou (2010), p. 3.
17. EC (2008), p. 81.
18. Central bank of Cyprus, 2010. The Pimco report on Cyprus made this observation on the Cypriot property market, 'A key feature of the Cyprus banking system has been the practice of pursuing asset-based lending, meaning a high reliance on collateral in the underwriting of loans, often with less attention paid to a borrower's ability to meet debt service payments on the loan. The strength of such an approach is noted in the observation that, "Under historically more normal economic conditions, this collateral-focused lending practice has served to protect Cyprus PIs from losses on seriously delinquent loans...Borrowers who were unable to meet their obligations could resolve their difficulties by selling property, releasing equity or pledging further collateral." However, it noted that, "With the collapse in the real estate market, these paths to resolution have effectively been closed and borrowers who are unable to meet their obligations are simply falling further into arrears.' PIMCO, 'Independent Due Diligence of the Banking System of Cyprus' (February 2013), p. 10.

    http://www.centralbank.gov.cy/media/pdf/CyprusIndependentDue DiligenceReport_18April.pdf
19. The descriptor is found on their website, at http://www.enasp.eu/eu-asisp-annual-national-reports-on-social-protection/
20. Petmesidou (2010), p. 24, http://socialprotection.eu/files_db/886/asisp_ANR10_Cyprus.pdf
21. https://www.imf.org/external/np/ms/2011/021511.htm. The report also said that, 'The ongoing risks in international financial markets call for a continuation of conservative balance sheet management and careful supervision.'
22. The party was founded as the Communist Party of Cyprus in 1926, setting as its aim - as described according to the history they present on their website – 'not only the struggle against exploitation but also the liberation of our country from British colonial yoke'. They subsequently 'laid down the foundations for the class-based workers movement connecting it from the beginning with the Marxist-Leninist outlook'. http://www.akel.org.cy/en/?p=1450#
23. Maria Petmesidou, 'Cyprus: Annual National Report 2010, Pensions, Health and Long-Term Care', *The European Commission* (May, 2010), p. 10, http://socialprotection.eu/files_db/886/asisp_ANR10_Cyprus.pdf
24. Maria Petmesidou, 'Cyprus: Annual National Report 2011, Pensions, Health and Long-Term Care', *The European Commission* (May, 2011), p. 18, http://socialprotection.eu/files_db/1100/asisp_ANR11_Cyprus.pdf
25. Op. cit., p. 3.
26. Cited in Athanasios Orphanides, 'What Happened in Cyprus? The Economic Consequences of the Last Communist Government in Europe', *MIT Sloan School of Management* (May 2014), pp. 7–8.

27. As was reported in *The Guardian* on the 29th July, 2011, available online at http://www.theguardian.com/business/2011/jul/29/european-debt-crisis-cyprus
28. From an interview with the authors on the June 4, 2014.
29. From an interview with the authors on June 30, 2014.
30. http://www.telegraph.co.uk/news/worldnews/europe/cyprus/8632718/Anger-grows-in-Cyprus-over-criminal-errors-behind-explosion.html
31. http://www.voanews.com/content/anger-grows-in-cyprus-over-muni tions-blast-125503253/167748.html
32. Orphanides, pp. 7–8.
33. http://www.reuters.com/article/2011/10/03/us-cyprus-blast-inquiry-idU STRE7921L920111003
34. http://www.bbc.co.uk/news/world-europe-15159826
35. 'Moody's Investment Service – Global Credit Research', July 27, 2001), https://www.moodys.com/research/Moodys-downgrades-Cyprus-to-Baa1-from-A2-negative-outlook?docid=PR_223439
36. Orphanides, p. 8.
37. http://www.spiegel.de/international/europe/greek-debt-crisis-how-gold man-sachs-helped-greece-to-mask-its-true-debt-a-676634.html
38. http://diepresse.com/home/wirtschaft/international/500632/Korruption-und-Steuerhinterziehung_Griechenland-versinkt-im-Sumpf- Christine Lagarde remarked in the summer of 2012, to much criticism, that she felt more sympathy with children in Africa than tax evaders in Greece.
39. European Commission, 'Report on Greek Government Deficit and Debt Statistics', January 2010, p. 4, pp. 27–28.
40. http://www.bloomberg.com/apps/news?pid=newsarchive&sid=aUi3XLU wIIVA
41. http://www.nytimes.com/2010/04/28/business/global/28drachma.html?_r=0, http://news.bbc.co.uk/1/hi/business/8647441.stm
42. From an IMF statement, published on the May 2, 20110, available online at http://www.imf.org/external/pubs/ft/survey/so/2010/car050210a.htm
43. http://www.nytimes.com/2010/05/06/world/europe/06greece.html?src=me&_r=0 and http://www.eubusiness.com/news-eu/greece-imf-finance.adn
44. http://www.marketwatch.com/story/ecb-suspends-rating-threshold-for-greek-debt-2010-05-03-3400
45. http://www.bloomberg.com/news/2011-06-13/greece-s-long-term-rating-cut-to-ccc-by-s-p-on-outlook-for-restructuring.html
46. http://www.european-council.europa.eu/home-page/highlights/a-common-response-to-the-crisis-situation.aspx?lang=en
47. According to data compiled by the World Bank: http://data.worldbank.org/indicator/NY.GDP.MKTP.KD.ZG
48. http://blogs.lse.ac.uk/greeceatlse/2012/03/23/are-the-european-banks-saving-greece-or-saving-themselves/#more-537
49. A summary of the summit meeting was published on October 26, 2011, and is available online at http://www.consilium.europa.eu/uedocs/cms_data/docs/pressdata/en/ec/125645.pdf

50. http://www.iif.com/press/press+239.php
51. http://online.wsj.com/news/articles/SB10001424052970204603004577271383829531576
52. http://www.bloombergview.com/articles/2012-03-12/credit-default-swap-time-bomb-failed-to-go-off-over-greece-view
53. http://online.wsj.com/news/articles/SB1000142412788732429910457852720278166700888
54. International Monetary Fund, 'Greece: Ex Post Evaluation of Exceptional Access under the 2010 Stand-By Arrangement, (Washington DC, June 2013), found at http://www.imf.org/external/pubs/ft/scr/2013/cr13156.pdf
55. Op. cit., p. 1.
56. Op. cit, pp. 22–23.
57. Op. cit. pp. 9–10.
58. http://www.nytimes.com/2012/02/21/world/europe/agreement-close-on-a-bailout-for-greece-european-finance-ministers-say.html
59. IMF (2013), p. 1.
60. Op. cit, p. 10.
61. http://online.wsj.com/news/articles/SB1000142412788732429910457852720278166700888
62. http://www.ft.com/cms/s/0/78ab958c-c4db-11e0-9c4d-00144feabdc0.html#axzz39oHfUSLk
63. http://online.wsj.com/news/articles/SB1000142412788732429910457852720278166700888
64. Macroeconomics forecasts by the European Commission, updated every quarter, found at http://ec.europa.eu/economy_finance/eu/countries/cyprus_en.htm
65. http://www.eunews.it/en/2014/01/27/the-troika-effect-european-unions-greece-lost-25-of-its-gdp/12218
66. This was not the only problem with the report. There appears to have been no co-ordination by PIMCO with the Central Bank of Cyprus, and no consideration of the potential sizeable fallout: in the words of Andreas Artemis, when giving evidence in his deposition to the Investigation Committee of the Economy, 'PIMCO refused persistently to discuss with the banks either the assumptions or the findings, despite repeated written requests from us to the governor, and our warnings that the rumoured overestimation would be catastrophic both for the banks and for the economy.' The somewhat extreme treatment of Cyprus by PIMCO was ironically acknowledged by the IMF, 'Furthermore, unlike previous exercises in peer countries, PIMCO has used a more conservative methodology in arriving at the final numbers.' See Artemis, 2013, and Orphanides p. 29.
67. PIMCO (2013), pp. 8–9.
68. 'Results of the 2011 EBA EU-wide stress test: Summary, Marfin Popular Bank Co Ltd', http://www.eba.europa.eu/documents/10180/15935/CY006.pdf/e2f3605e-359a-4519-b15b-296ba0d0d2fd. For the opening statement of the tests in general, which includes an overview and

account of their methodology, see Andrea Enria, 'Publication of the 2011 EU-wide Stress Test Results' published on July 15, 2011, available online at http://www.eba.europa.eu/documents/10180/15935/Opening+statement+-+Andrea+Enria+-+FINAL.pdf/d0024654-e56a-4263-b587-3e691565dc3a

69. 'The European Banking Authority 2011 EU-Wide Stress Test Aggregate Report' published on July 15, 2011, see http://www.eba.europa.eu/documents/10180/15935/EBA_ST_2011_Summary_Report_v6.pdf/54a9e c8e-3a44-449f-9a5f-e820cc2c2f0a p. 36, for the sample list. This statement is found on p. 31, 'The EBA undertakes a regular risk assessment on a sample of thirty banks in the EU. The sample of banks is based on a combination of asset size, cross border importance, use of IRB [Internal Ratings Based] models'.

70. 'Results of the 2011 EBA EU-wide stress test: Summary, Piraeus Bank', p.6, http://www.eba.europa.eu/documents/10180/15935/GR033.pdf/b8f02648-4beb-4efa-8d61-f02acbc5b666

71. From a transcripted interview with the authors.

72. Demetriades (2012), p. 1.

73. From an interview with the authors on June 2, 2014.

74. From an interview with the authors on the June 4 and September 15, 2014.

75. http://www.parikia.co.uk/daily-news/cyprus-news/cyprus-news-in-english/44214-shiarly-we-made-two-big-mistakes.html

76. Orphanides, p. 26.

77. Op. cit., p. 34.

78. Interview with the authors on June 7, 2014.

79. Engelen, p. 51.

80. Prior to that, Demetriades was Professor of Financial Economics at the University of Leicester. The majority of his papers before attending public office appear concerned with the relationship between financial development and economic growth. For example, 'Financial Development and Economic Growth: Assessing the Evidence', *The Economic Journal*, C (1997), and 'Financial Restraints in the South Korean Miracle', *Journal of Development Economics*, LXIV, 2001.

81. A highly critical, and strongly phrased, editorial of the Cyprus Mail by ex-governor Orphanides described Demetriades as the man who 'heads the government's offensive against the banks'. As it continued, 'The banks...are facing a hostile government which is doing everything in its power to discredit the banking sector in order to deflect attention away from its responsibilities for the huge problems facing the country.' Cited in Oprhanides, p. 23.

82. 'Cyprus Financial Crisis: the framework for an economic recovery within the eurozone'. Speech by Panicos Demetriades, Governor of the Central Bank of Cyprus, at a discussion organised by the Hellenic American Bankers Association and the Cyprus-US Chamber of Commerce (New York, December 11, 2012).

83. The statement, published January 13, 2012, is available online at http://www.standardandpoors.com/ratings/articles/en/us/?article Type=HTML&assetID=1245327297152.

    The S&P report also noted that 'we believe that a reform process based on a pillar of fiscal austerity alone risks becoming self-defeating, as domestic demand falls in line with consumers' rising concerns about job security and disposable incomes, eroding national tax revenues.'

84. As covering in the report entitled 'The Cyprus Economy', by the Bank of Cyprus Group Economic Research Divison, published July 2012, pp. 7–8.

85. Section 2.2, Article 2:4 of the regulation states that 'exposure to European Union Member States central governments or central banks denominated and funded in the domestic currency of the Member State concerned shall be assigned a risk weight of 0%.' See http://www.toezicht.dnb.nl/en/binaries/51-217627.pdf

86. For more on 2010 Basel rules on global regulatory standards for bank capital, see 'Capital Requirements – CRD IV/CRR, Frequently Asked Questions', http://europa.eu/rapid/press-release_MEMO-13-690_en.htm

87. http://www.reuters.com/article/2014/03/10/eurozone-banks-idUSL6N0M 717020140310

88. See for example 'Over the Counter Derivatives Markets and the Commodity Exchange Act' (November 1999), p. 1, published online at http://www.treasury.gov/resource-center/fin-mkts/documents/otcact.pdf

89. Summarising a 2013 disposition to the Cypriot Parliament while in conversation with the authors of this book.

90. From an interview with the authors on the June 4, 2014.

91. European Central Bank, 'Annual Report' (March 7, 2000), available online at http://www.ecb.europa.eu/pub/pdf/annrep/ar1999en.pdf

92. The evidence for this comes from the marking of €3.8 billion assets on the April 2012 balance sheet of the Central Bank of Cyprus as 'Other claims on euro area credit institutions denominated in euro', which is frequently 'code' for ELA funding.

    See http://www.centralbank.gov.cy/media/pdf/BALANCE_SHEET_ APRIL_2012_EN.pdf for the data, and an FT investigation, 'Buiter on Europe's secret liquidity operations', *Financial Times* (January 24, 2011), available at http://ftalphaville.ft.com//2011/01/24/466731/buiter-on-europes-secret-liquidity-operations/

93. *Der Spiegel*, 'Banks on the Brink: ECB May Cut Emergency Funding to Cyprus' (March 20, 2013), available online at http://www.spiegel.de/international/europe/ecb-may-cut-emergency-funding-to-cypriot-banks-after-refusal-a-889967.html This period of the crisis is discussed in more detail in chapter four.

94. Sarris has this thought on this decision: 'For political reasons, the government did not want to take on the political cost of seeking assistance from the Troika. Instead we sought money from the Russians and got a loan of €2.5 billion which further increased the insecurity of the capital markets'.

95. http://www.ft.com/cms/s/655a3fd2-de31-11e0-9fb7-00144feabdc0,
    Authorised=false.html?_i_location=http%3A%2F%2Fwww.ft.com%2
    Fcms%2Fs%2F0%2F655a3fd2-de31-11e0-9fb7-00144feabdc0.html%3Fsit
    eedition%3Duk&siteedition=uk&_i_referer=http%3A%2F%2Fen.
    wikipedia.org%2Fwiki%2F2012%25E2%2580%259313_Cypriot_
    financial_crisis
96. From an interview with the authors on the June 4, 2014.
97. http://www.ft.com/cms/s/0/e1ecbb44-109c-11e2-a5f7-00144feabdc0.
    html
98. http://www.bbc.co.uk/news/business-18577951
99. From an interview with the authors on the June 4, 2014

# 4  Bailouts and Bail-Ins

1. At around thirty billion dollars, the GDP of Cyprus is approximately
   one-tenth of Greece.
2. Transcript from a meeting with the authors on the June 3, 2014.
3. http://worldnews.about.com/od/cyprus/qt/What-Theyre-Saying-About-
   Cyprus.htm
4. http://www.international-economy.com/TIE_Sp13_Engelen.pdf
5. http://www.spiegel.de/international/europe/german-intelligence-report-
   warns-cyprus-not-combating-money-laundering-a-865451.html
6. For more on this see the IMF Statement on the crisis of the 24th March,
   2013, available online at https://www.imf.org/external/np/sec/pr/2013/
   pr1391.htm. See also http://dealbreaker.com/2013/03/cyprus-was-the-
   template-for-all-future-european-bank-bailouts-for-a-whole-
   afternoon/
7. Klaus C. Engelen, 'From Deauville to Cyprus', *The Magazine of International Economic Policy* (2013), pp. 50–53, 73–76.
8. Transcript from the interview of June 4, 2014.
9. Ollie Rehn, 'Statement on Cyprus in the European Parliament',
   Strasbourg, April 17,2013, published online at http://europa.eu/rapid/
   press-release_SPEECH-13-325_en.htm
10. From a transcripted meeting with author on the June 4, 2014.
11. http://www.theguardian.com/business/2013/mar/24/eurozone-crisis-
    cyprus-bailout-eurogroup-meeting
12. 'Memorandum of Understanding on Specific Economic Policy
    Conditionality', published April 12, 2013, available online at http://
    www.naftemporiki.gr/cmsutils/downloadpdf.aspx?id=647166
13. http://ec.europa.eu/finance/bank/crisis_management/index_en.htm#
    framework2012
14. http//Eurozone.europa.eu/newsroom/news/2013/03/eg-statement-
    cyprus-25-03-13/
15. 'The Economic Adjustment programme for Cyprus', European Commis-
    sion, May 17, 2013, published online at http://ec.europa.eu/economy_
    finance/publications/occasional_paper/2013/pdf/ocp149_enpdf

16. 'Cyprus: Anti-Money Laundering and Combating the Financing of Terrorism', a report published on the 27th September 2011, available online at http://www.coe.int/t/dghl/monitoring/moneyval/Evaluations/round4/CYP4_MER_MONEYVAL%282011%292_en.pdf
17. The main legislation governing Company Law in Cyprus is the Cyprus Companies Law, Cap.113 of 1951.
18. From an interview with the authors on June 4, 2014.
19. Treaty of Establishment, Article 23, states that 'every person or jointly with others has the right to acquire own, possess ,enjoy or dispose of any movable or immovable property and has the right to respect for such right, no deprivation or restriction or limitation of any such right shall be made, except as provided in this article'.
20. The Court thus concluded that any rights of the depositors of Laiki, if affected by the sale of the Laiki assets, do not fall within the ambit of the jurisdiction of the Supreme Court, which cannot review the legitimacy of the decree but can be examined in the course of civil actions in the civil courts.
21. http://www.cdr-news.com/categories/economics/cyprus:-the-post-bailout-battle
22. 'IMF Statement on Cyprus', published March 24, 2013, available online at https://www.imf.org/external/np/sec/pr/2013/pr1391.htm
23. Triantafyillides, Advocate for Shareholders of the Bank of Cyprus: Transcript of meeting held on June 4, 2014.
24. http://www.keeptalkinggreece.com/2013/03/21/irish-mep-calls-olli-rehn-to-resign-over-cyprus-bailout-fiasco/
25. Comments reprinted online at http://sharonbowles.org.uk/en/article/2013/671744/the-cyprus-bailout-deal-is-a-disaster-for-eu-rules-and-single-market-principles-bowles
26. http://www.bbc.co.uk/news/world-europe-22183867
27. From an article in *The Economist* entitled 'Unfair, short-sighted and self-defeating', published March 16 2013, available online at http://www.economist.com/blogs/schumpeter/2013/03/cyprus-bail-out
28. https://citizenactionmonitor.wordpress.com/2013/03/28/events-in-cyprus-expose-eu-plan-to-steal-peoples-savings-and-bailout-private-banks/
29. http://www.cnbc.com/id/100575889
30. http://www.telegraph.co.uk/finance/debt-crisis-live/9939296/Cyprus-bail-out-as-it-happened-March-19-2013.html
31. George Osborne at a Treasury committee hearing, http://www.bbc.co.uk/news/business-21936366
32. http://www.standard.co.uk/news/uk/cyprus-troops-will-be-compensated-8537980.html
33. http://www.acb.com.cy/cgibin/hweb?-A=159&-V=codes
34. http://www.bridgingandcommercial.co.uk/article-desc-3041_brits-spared#.U_OCVGPp9bo
35. As discussed in chapter 3.

36. From the Press Release Archive of the European Commission, April 13, published online at http://ec.europa.eu/ireland/press_office/media_centre/apr2013_en.htm
37. Caritas Europe, 'The European Crisis and its Human Cost', 2014 report, published online at http://www.caritas.eu/sites/default/files/caritascrisisreport_2014_en.pdf
38. 'Policy Area: Lessons from Cyprus', published by the European Union Center of North Carolina, available online at europe.unc.edu/wp-content/uploads/2013/09/Brief1308-cyprus.pdf.
39. Transcript from an interview held with the authors on June 2, 2014.
40. Transcript from an interview held with the authors on June 1, 2014.
41. Transcript from an interview held with the authors on June, 2 2014.
42. From a speech by Delia Velculescu at The Economist Conference, entitled 'Cyprus on the Mend?', November 25, 2013, published online at http://online.wsj.com/news/articles/SB10001424127887324492604579082843940362678
43. Many other borrowers in countries in Poland, Hungary and the Baltics had also taken out Swiss franc loans.
44. Transcript from an interview held with the authors on September 10, 2014.
45. http://www.expatsblog.com/news/0107146185/-cyprus-expats-get-settlement-on-mortgage-misselling-scandal#sthash.y48skGJM.dpuf
46. Transcript from an interview held with the authors on June 2, 2014.
47. http://www.spiegel.de/international/europe/troika-rejects-plan-in-cyprus-to-tap-pension-funds-a-890394.html
48. Transcript from an interview held with the authors on June 2, 2014.
49. For those employed prior to the new arrangements, the lump sum and the pension they receive upon retirement would be calculated under a two-pillar formula. The first was based on whatever had been accumulated up to December 2012. For those cases there was no change. All pension rights accumulated until the end of 2012 would also have no change but from January 1, 2013 onwards the pension would be based on the average of what they earn form January 1, 2013 until the day of their retirement. If someone retires on January 1, 2033 then it would be the average of this 20 years plus what they earn until 2012 .
50. www.ibtimes.co.uk/cyprus-greece-piraeus
51. http://www.parikiaki.com/2013/05/sale-of-greek-branches-of-cypriot-banks-was-set-out-by-troika/
52. http://www.ekathimerini.com/4dcgi/_w_articles_wsite2_1_26/03/2013_489921 The deal meant that Piraeus Bank had consolidated total assets of 95 billion euros, 1,660 branches and 24,000 employees.
53. http://www.parikiaki.com/2013/05/sale-of-greek-branches-of-cypriot-banks-was-set-out-by-troika/
54. http://www.piraeusbank.ua/en/bank_news.html?_m=publications&_c=view&_t=rec&id=790
55. http://news.bbc.co.uk/1/hi/business/7626624.stm
56. As discussed in chapter 3.

57. http://famagusta-gazette.com/piraeus-bank-acquires-the-greek-operations-of-cypriot-banks-p18716-69.htm
58. http://uk.reuters.com/article/2013/03/26/piraeusbank-cyprus-idUSL5N0CI0D420130326
59. From transcript of meeting with the authors, summarising information provided in an affidavit to the Cyprus parliamentary Finance committee dealing with matters relating to the financial crisis (the original 44-page document is written in Greek).
60. http://www.parikiaki.com/2013/05/sale-of-greek-branches-of-cypriot-banks-was-set-out-by-troika/ The CBC governor also estimated insured deposits in the Greek branches to total around 9 billion euros.
61. Transcript from an interview held with the authors on June 4, 2014.
62. In December 2008, the Irish Government put €5.5 billion into the banking sector.
63. Credit Institutions (Financial Support) Act 2008 of the Irish Parliament; Credit Institutions (Eligible Liabilities) Guarantee Scheme 2009.
64. http://www.washingtonpost.com/wp-dyn/content/article/2010/11/28/AR2010112804133.htm
65. http://elpais.com/elpais/2013/03/16/opinion/1363462478_488567.html
66. http://www.scribd.com/doc/188183271/Before-2008
67. In 2005 Spain built more apartments and houses than in France, Germany and UK combined.
68. http://www.nytimes.com/2012/11/29/business/global/european-commission-approves-bailout-of-four-spanish-banks.html?_r=0
69. http://www.ft.com/cms/s/0/b1cfa4a0-92e1-11e1-aa60-00144feab49a.html
70. www.bloombergbriefs.com+04%2F04%2F2013+cyprus
71. http://www.bbc.co.uk/news/world-europe-22058565
72. http://www.spiegel.de/international/europe/luxembourg-warns-of-investor-flight-from-europe-a-891672.html.
73. http://www.spiegel.de/international/europe/tax-haven-reputation-plagues-eu-bailout-of-cyprus-a-877369.html
74. http://www.spiegel.de/international/europe/german-intelligence-report-warns-cyprus-not-combating-money-laundering-a-865451.html
75. http://www.zerohedge.com/news/2013-04-03/putin-offers-3-month-offshore-tax-cheat-amnesty-there-can-be-no-untouchables
76. http://www.nytimes.com/2013/04/04/opinion/cyprus-a-blessing-for-russia-in-disguise.html?pagewanted=all
77. http://www.bloomberg.com/news/2011-12-23/cyprus-russia-sign-2-5-billion-euro-loan-deal-in-moscow-1-.html
78. http://www.bloomberg.com/news/2013-03-21/cyprus-said-to-seek-about-5-billion-euro-russian-loan-in-moscow.html
79. Transcript of meeting held with the authors on June 3, 2014.
80. As discussed in chapter 2

## 5   Economic Recovery and Strategic Challenges

1. See for example Ben Bernanke, 'The Macroeconomics of the Great Depression: A Comparative Approach', *Journal of Money, Credit, and Banking* (Blackwell Publishing), XXVII, pp. 1–28. and Steve Keen, 'Finance and economic breakdown: modelling Minsky's Financial Instability Hypothesis', *Journal of Post Keynesian Economics*, XVII, pp. 607–635.
2. For the pledge see http://news.bbc.co.uk/1/hi/business/6999615.stm, and the nationalisation, http://www.theguardian.com/business/2008/feb/17/northernrock.nationalisation
3. The term has precedents stretching back to the 18<sup>th</sup> century, though its modern usage is normally attributed to Walter Bagehot in the 1870s, for which see Walter Bagehot *Lombard Street: A Description of the Money Market* (London: NuVision (ori. pub. 1873), 2008), pp. 30–32. See also T. Humphrey, 'Lender of last resort: the concept in history', *Economic Review*, LXXV, pp. 8–16.
4. For which see T. Curry and L. Shibut (eds.), 'The Cost of the Savings and Loan Crisis', *FDIC Banking Review*, XIII (2000), pp. 26–35.
5. Rehn (2013)
6. http://www.telegraph.co.uk/finance/financialcrisis/10655816/Stoic-Cyprus-back-from-the-dead-after-banking-collapse.html.
7. Panos Pashardes and Nicoletta Pashaourtidou, 'Output Loss from the Banking Crisis in Cyprus', *Cyprus Economic Policy Review* (VII), pp. 3–24.
8. The Ernst & Young report is published online at http://www.ey.com/Publication/vwLUAssets/EY-Eurozone-Sep-2014-Cyprus/$FILE/EY-Eurozone-Sep-2014-Cyprus.pdf
9. Anon, *EY: Outlook for Cyprus* (Oxford Economics, 2014), pp. 1–3.
10. Transcript of meeting on June 6, 2014.
11. See the Address by Minister of Finance Harris Georgiades, Brussels Breakfast Event, December 9, 2013, http://www.mof.gov.cy/mof/mof.nsf/All/C5768DB684C30FADC2257C40003201D1/$file/Brussels%20Breakfast%20Event.pdf, pp. 2–3.
12. Op. cit., pp. 1–2.
13. Valculescu (2013). http://www.imf.org/external/np/speeches/2013/112513.htm.
14. http://uk.reuters.com/article/2014/07/02/uk-cyprus-imf-idUKKBN0F71GA20140702
15. http://www.news.cyprus-property-buyers.com/2014/11/01/troika-discuss-insolvency-framework/id=0040719.
16. MoU version 12 April 2013 Q4 2013 check updated version 'Memorandum of Understanding on Specific Economic Policy Conditionality', published 12 April 2013, available online at http://www.naftemporiki.gr/cmsutils/downloadpdf.aspx?id=647166
17. http://www.financialmirror.com/news-details.php?nid=32342
18. Data from the 'World Travel and Tourism Economic Impact Report on Cyprus', World Travel and Tourism Council, 2014.
19. http://cyprusair.com/871,0,0,0,2-Shareholder-StructureCapital.aspx

20. Memorandum of Understanding (April 2013).
21. From a transcript interview with the authors on November 24, 2014.
22. http://www.vedomosti.ru/finance/news/28979121/kiprskij-diskont
23. http://www.telegraph.co.uk/finance/newsbysector/energy/oilandgas/106
    47382/Gas-bonanza-for-Cyprus-hostage-to-strategic-battle-with-Turkey.
    html
24. http://www.rigzone.com/news/oil_gas/a/124230/Israel_Firms_Invest_In_
    US_Energy_Search_Off_Cyprus#sthash.7tCuUrGl.dpuf.
25. Estimates of up to ten billion euros.
26. http://www.turkishweekly.net/news/173101/turkey-warns-greek-cyprus-
    over-hydrocarbon-searches.html
27. As discussed in interview by the authors with George Pantelides on the
    November 24, 2014.
28. http://uk.reuters.com/article/2014/07/02/uk-cyprus-imf-idUKKBN0F71GA
    20140702
29. Referred to as a 'wasted chance' in the British newspaper *The
    Telegraph* http://www.telegraph.co.uk/finance/financialcrisis/10655816/
    Stoic-Cyprus-back-from-the-dead-after-banking-collapse.html
30. http://www.telegraph.co.uk/finance/newsbysector/energy/oilandgas/106
    47382/Gas-bonanza-for-Cyprus-hostage-to-strategic-battle-with-Turkey.
    html
31. Turkey would itself benefit if a pipeline was connected to its territory for
    carrying gas/oil to Europe.
32. http://www.ihsmaritime360.com/article/13183/cyprus-shipping-sector-
    hits-5-1-of-gdp
33. https://www.pwc.com.cy/en/industries/assets/pwc-cy_Cyprus-Shipping
    10. pdf
34. Transcript of a meeting with the authors on June 6, 2014.

# 6   Bail-In and the Future of the Eurozone

1. Robert Pringle, *The Money Trap* (London: Palgrave Macmillan, 2014),
   p. 92. Palgrave Macmillan 2012. He offers the further observation that,
   'The Euro transformed balance of payments problems into sovereign
   debt problems which in some ways were harder to resolve', Op. cit.,
   p. 104.
2. Op. cit., p. 92.
3. http://www.bloombergview.com/articles/2012-05-23/merkel-should-
   know-her-country-has-been-bailed-out-too
4. stats.**oecd**.org/Index.aspx?**Data**SetCode%3DANHRS
5. Examples abound, but a representative image of such attitudes can be
   found in William Lecky's *A history of European Morals from Augustus to
   Charlemagne*, 2 vols. (London, 1869), II, p. 13,
   'Of that Byzantine empire, the universal verdict of history is that it
   constitutes, without a single exception, the most thoroughly base and
   despicable form that civilization has yet assumed. There has been no

other enduring civilization so absolutely destitute of all forms and elements of greatness, and none to which the epithet "mean" may be so emphatically applied... The history of the empire is a monotonous story of the intrigues of priests, eunuchs, and women, of poisonings, of conspiracies, of uniform ingratitude.'

6. Joseph Stiglitz (in *The Guardian*, 17 August 2012) argued that 'No large economy has ever recovered from a downturn as a result of austerity. It is a certain recipe for exacerbating the recession and inflicting unnecessary pain on the economy. Any additional spending should address the longer term problems – inequality and industrial restructuring – and target the neediest in society who, because of the downturn, are suffering the most. A more progressive tax structure – higher taxes at the top, lower taxes at the bottom – would stimulate the economy. Taxing the excessive speculation that goes on in the financial sector would also be a good thing.'

7. From an interview with the authors on July 4, 2014. They add the further statement that 'there are numerous cases where three generations of families are in effect being supported by the grandparents who themselves live on reduced pensions of €500 per month.'

8. When, on May 6, 2011, *Der Spiegel* reported that the Greek government was threatening to stop using the euro, the currency suffered its worst two-day plunge since December 2008. The report is available online at http://www.spiegel.de/international/europe/athens-mulls-plans-for-new-currency-greece-considers-exit-from-euro-zone-a-761201.html

9. For more on this subject see Mark Weisbrot and Luis Sandoval, 'Argentina's Economic Recovery: Policy Choices and Implications', published by the Centre for Economic and Policy Research, October 2007.

10. The European Commission report 'Proposal for a Single Resolution Mechanism for the Banking Union, published on the July 10, 2013, available online at http://europa.eu/rapid/press-release_MEMO-13-675_en.htm.

11. From the Economic and Financial Affairs Council report, 'Single resolution mechanism: Council reviews the state of play of the negotiations,' published February 18, 2014. The report also suggests 'more closely regulated oversight of the SRB over national resolution authorities' and a central role for the European Central Bank in determining whether a banking institution is failing or likely to fail, while the SRB should ultimately maintain a possibility to effectively influence that decision too.' Available online at http://consilium.europa.eu/homepage/showfocus?focus Name=single-resolution-mechanism-council-reviews-the-state-of-play-of-the-negotiations&lang=en.

12. http://www.cnbc.com/id/102072762#

13. He expands on this point further, 'My prediction is not that the euro will fall apart, but that it leads to a stagnation and animosity even more than we see today among the people of Europe,' he said. 'You see this very strongly in southern Europe, where people face this mass unemployment, in France, where Marine le Pen in the polls has the strongest

party and with Syriza in Greece which is presenting radical decisions and has the most support in the polls.'

14. http://www.project-syndicate.org/commentary/george-soros-maps-the-terrain-of-a-global-economy-that-is-increasingly-shaped-by-china.
15. http://rt.com/business/euro-economy-draghi-stability-402/
16. 'The Scope of monetary policy' as defined by the ECB, available online at http://www.ecb.europa.eu/mopo/intro/role/html/index.en.html.
17. http://www.dw.de/imf-calls-for-new-growth-momentum/a-17987184.
18. http://www.imf.org/external/pubs/ft/scr/2013/cr13241.pdf
19. http://www.imf.org/external/pubs/cat/longres.aspx?sk=40820.0.
20. http://online.wsj.com/articles/greek-economy-grows-for-first-time-in-six-years-1415962022
21. Key data indicators for the Euro area, up to November 2014 are found at http://ec.europa.eu/economy_finance/db_indicators/key_indicators/documents/key_indicators_en.pdf

## Conclusion

1. http://www.ft.com/cms/s/0/4db45c9c-7f95-11e4-b4f5-00144feabdc0.html#axzz3Lxt5XLDc
2. From the Eurostat employment figures from the European Commission, for which see http://ec.europa.eu/eurostat/statistics-explained/index.php/Main_Page
3. As discussed in chapter five.

# Bibliography

Adams, T. W. and Cottrell, A. J. *Cyprus between East and West* (Baltimore, John Hopkins Press, 1968).

Alastos, Doros. *Cyprus in History* (London: Zeno, 1976).

Attalides, Michael. *Cyprus: Nationalism and International Politics* (Edinburgh: Q Press, 1979).

Averoff-Tossizza, Evangelos. *Lost Opportunities: The Cyprus Question*, 1950–63 (New York, Aristide Publishing, 1986).

Bailey, Sydney. *The Procedure of the United Nations Security Council* (Oxford: Clarendon Press, 1975).

Barker, Dudley. *Grivas, Portrait of a Terrorist* (London: Cresset Press, 1959).

Barros, James. *The United Nations Past, Present and Future* (London: Collier-Macmillan Ltd, 1972).

Bartlett, Margaret W. *Cyprus, The United Nations and the Quest for Unity* (Cambridge: Melrose Books, 2007).

Bowett, David. *United Nations Forces* (London: Stevens and Sons, 1964).

Brewin, Christopher. *European Union and Cyprus* (Huntingdon: Eothen Press, 2000).

Brownlie, Ian. *Basic Documents in International Law* (Oxford: Clarendon Press, 1975).

Buiter, Willem. 'The Icelandic Banking Crisis and What to Do about It', Centre for Economic Policy Research (October 2008), available online at http://www.cepr.org/pubs/PolicyInsights/ CEPR_Policy_Insight_026.asp

Cable, Vince. *The Storm: The World Economic Crisis and What It Means* (London: Atlantic Books, 2009).

Casaca, Paulo. 'Bail in Replacing Bail out', Euro-Reform 2014 Initiative, Press Release February 19, 2014.

Cassese, Antonio. *Legal Essays on United Nations Peacekeeping* (The Netherlands: Sijhoff and Noordhoff, 1978).

Clerides, Glafkos. *Cyprus, My Deposition* (Nicosia: Alithia, 1989–1992).

Congdon, Tim. *Money in a Free Society* (New York: Encounter Books, 2011).

Constantinou, Marios. 'Constitutional Learning for Cypriots in the Light of the Swiss and EU Experience; Theoretical and Practical Stakes of federalisation', *The Cyprus Review*, XV (2002), pp. 13–65.

Cordier, A. and Foote, W. *Public Papers of the Secretary-General of the United Nations*, 1960–1970 (New York: Columbia University Press, 1975).

Cordier, A. and Harrelson, M. *Public Papers of the Secretary-General of the United Nations*, 1965–67 (New York, Columbia University Press, 1976).

Coufoudakis, Van. *Essays on the Cyprus conflict* (Location Pella Publishing, 1976).

Coufoudakis, V. and Kyriakides, K. *The Case against the Annan Plan* (London: Wharf Mill, 2004).

Coughlan, R. 'From Corporate Autonomy to the Search for Territorial Federalism', in Guy, Y. (ed.), *Autonomy and Ethnicity: Negotiating Completing Claims in Multi-Ethnic States* (Cambridge: Cambridge University Press, 1999).

Couloumbis, Theodore & Hicks, Sally (eds), 'US Foreign Policy Toward Greece and Cyprus', *Conference Proceedings, Centre for Mediterranean Studies and American Hellenic Institute* (1975).

Crawford, James, Hafner, Gerhard and Pellet, Alain, 'Does the Treaty of Lausanne 1923 Confer on Turkey Any Specific Rights with Respect to Cyprus?' in Markides, Alecos (ed.), *Cyprus and the European Union Membership* (Nicosia, 2002).

Denktash, Rauf. *Cyprus: The Need for New Perspectives; Rauf Denktash at the United Nations* (Huntingdon: Eothen Press, 2002).

Diez Thomas, and Tocci, Nathalie. *Cyprus: A Conflict at the Crossroads* (Manchester: Manchester University Press, 2009).

Dodd, Clement H. *The Cyprus Issue* (Huntingdon: Eothen Press, 1995).

Ertekun, Necati Munir, 'The Turkish Cypriot Outlook', in Dodd, Clement H. (ed), *The Cyprus Issue: The Need for New Perspectives* (Huntingdon: Eothen Press, 1999).

Fabian, L. *Soldiers Without Enemies: Preparing the United Nations for Peacekeeping* (Washington: The Brookings Institute, 1971).

Ferguson, Niall. *The Cash Nexus: Money and Power in the Modern World, 1700–2000* (London: Penguin, 2001).

Filardo, Andrew. *The Impact of the International Financial Crisis on Asia and the Pacific: Highlighting Monetary Policy Challenges from a Negative Asset Price Bubble Perspective* (BIS Papers, 2011).

Foley, Charles. *Island in Revolt* (London: Longmans, 1962).

Foot, Hugh. *A Start in Freedom* (London: Hodder and Stoughton, 1964).

Fouskas, Vassilis and Tackie, Alex. *The Post Imperial Constitution* (Gloucester: Pluto Press, 2009).

Fouskas, Vassilis and Richter, Heinz. A. *Cyprus and Europe: The Long Way Back* (Mannheim: Bibliopolis, 2003).

Friedman, Seth. *Binge Trading: The Real Inside Story of Cash, Cocaine and Corruption in the City* (London: Penguin Books, 2009).

Gazioglou, Ahmet C. *Two Equal and Sovereign Peoples: A documented background to the Cyprus problem and the concept of partnership* (Nicosia: Cyprus Republic, 1997).

Gordenker, L. *The United Nations in International Politics* (Princeton, Princeton University Press, 1971).

Gregoriou, George. *Cyprus: A View from the Diaspora* (Smyrna Press, 2000).

Grivas, George. *Memoirs of General Grivas* (London: Longman, 1964).

Hannay, Lord David. *Cyprus: The Search for a Solution* (London: I.B. Taurus, 2004).

Higgins, R. *The Development of International Law through the Political Organs of the United Nations* (Oxford: Oxford University Press, 1963).

Higgins, R. *United Nations Peace Keeping 1946–67 Documents and Commentary* (Oxford: Oxford University Press, 1969).

Hill, George. *A History of Cyprus* (Cambridge: Cambridge University Press, 2010).

Hill, Sir George. *A History of Cyprus* (4 Vols) (Cambridge, Cambridge University Press, 1940–1952).

Hirsch, Fred. *Money International* (London: Penguin, 1969).

Hitchens, Christopher. Hostage to History: *Cyprus from the Ottomans to Kissinger* (London: Verso (orig. pub. 1984), 1997).

Holland, Robert. *Britain and the Revolt in Cyprus 1954–1959* (Oxford: Oxford University Press 1998).

Issing, Otmar. *The Birth of the Euro* (Cambridge: Cambridge University Press, 2008).

James, A. *The Politics of Peacekeeping* (London: Chatto and Windus, 1969).

Joseph, Josef S. *Cyprus: Ethnic Conflict and International Politics* (London: St Martin's Press, 1997).

Koumoulides, John T.A. (ed). *Cyprus in Transition* (London: Trigraph, 1986).

Lindley, Dan. 'The Military Factor in the Eastern Mediterranean', in Dodd, Clement H. (ed).*Cyprus: The Need for New Perspectives,* (Huntingdon: Eothen Press 1999).

Luard, E. *The United Nations* (London: Macmillan Press, 1979).

Mallinson, William. *Cyprus: A Modern History* (London: I. B. Tauris, 2008).

Marsh, David. *The Euro: The Politics of the New Global Currency* (New York: Yale University Press, 2009).

Mayes, Stanley. *Makarios: A Biography* (London: Macmillan, 1981).

Moran, Michael. *Cyprus: A European Anomaly* (Istanbul: Kindle Edition 2011).

O'Malley, Brendan and Craig, Ian. *The Cyprus Conspiracy* (London: I.B. Tauris, 2001).

Pantelis, Stavros. *A History of Cyprus* (London: East-West Publications, 2000).

Papadakis, Yiannis. *Divided Cyprus* (Indiana: Indiana University Press, 2006).

Pentzopoulos, Dimitris. *The Balkan Exchange of Minorities and Its Impact Upon Greece* (Paris: Mouton & Co, 1962).

Polyviou, Polyvios G. *The Tragedy and the Challenge* (Cyprus, 1975).

Polyviou, Polyvios G. *Cyprus in Search of Constitution* (Nicosia: Nicolaou & Sons Ltd, 1976).

Porter, A. N. and Stockwell, A.J. *British Imperial Policy and Decolonisation 1938–1964* (London: Macmillan, 1987).

Pringle, Robert. *The Money Trap* (London: Palgrave Macmillan, 2012).

Reddaway, John. *Burdened with Cyprus: The British Connection* (Weidenfeld and Nicolson: 1986).

Richard, Oliver P. *Mediating in Cyprus* (London: Portland, 1999).

Rogoff, Kenneth. *The Global Fallout of a Eurozone Collapse* (Financial Times, October 4, 2011).

Seyersted, Finn. *United Nations Forces in the Law of Peace and War* (The Netherlands, Sijjthoff-Leyden, 1972).

Seymour, Hersh. *The Price of Power: Kissinger in the Nixon White House* (London: Summit Books, 1983).

Sonyel, Salahi R. *Cyprus: Destruction of a Republic: British Documents, 1960–65* (Huntingdon: Eothen Press, 1997).

Sonyel, Salahi R. 'New Light On the Genesis of the Conflict', in Dodd, Clement H. (ed.). *Cyprus: The Need for New Perspectives* (Huntingdon: Eothen Press, 1999).

Svolopoulos, Konstantinos. *Greek Foreign Policy, 1945–1981* (Estia: Athens, 2002).

Theodhoropoulos, V., Lagkakos, E., Papoulias and Tzounis, T., *Reflections and Considerations about our Foreign Policy* (Athens, 1995).

Tocci, Nathalie. *EU Accession Dynamics and Conflict Resolution – Catalysing Peace or Consolidating Partition in Cyprus?* (London: Ashgate Publishing Ltd, 2004).

Trimikliniotis, Nicos and Bozkurt, Umut (eds.). *Beyond a Divided Cyprus*: *A State and Society in Transformation* (London: Palgrave Macmillan, 2012).

Tunkin, G. *Theory of International Law*, Vol. 12 (Washington DC: Dept. of State Publication, 1971).

Vanezis, P.N. *Makarios: Life and Leadership* (London: Abelard-Schuman, 1979).

Varnava, Andrekos, and Faustmann, Herbet (eds.). *Reunifying Cyprus: The Annan Plan & Beyond* (London: I.B. Tauris, 2009).

Yakinthos, Christalla. *Political Settlements in Divided Societies: Consociationalism and Cyprus* (London: Palgrave Macmillan, 2009).

## Articles

Bank of Cyprus Group Economic Research Divison, Report entitled 'The Cyprus Economy', published July 2012, pp. 7–8.

'Banks on the Brink: ECB May Cut Emergency Funding to Cyprus', *Der Spiegel* (March 20, 2013), available online at http://www.spiegel.de/international/europe/ecb-may-cut-emergency-funding-to-cypriot-banks-after-refusal-a-889967.html.

Bernanke, Ben. 'The Macroeconomics of the Great Depression: A Comparative Approach', *Journal of Money, Credit, and Banking* , XXVII (1995), pp. 1–28.

Bleicher, S. 'Legal Significance of Re-citation of General Assembly Resolutions', *American Journal of International Law*, LXIII (1969), pp. 444–478.

'Buiter on Europe's secret liquidity operations', *Financial Times* (January 24, 2011), available online at http://ftalphaville.ft.com//2011/01/24/466731/buiter-on-europes-secret-liquidity-operations/.

Caritas Europe, 'The European Crisis and its Human Cost', 2104 report, published online at http://www.caritas.eu/sites/default/files/caritascrisisreport_2014_en.pdf.

Central Bank of Cyprus, Economic Research. 'Concise Monetary Policy Report', February 2005.

'Concise Monetary Policy Report', the Central Bank of Cyprus, Economic Research Department, published February 2005.

Criton, Tornaritis. (Attorney- General of the Republic of Cyprus), Consti-tutional and Legal Problems in the Republic of Cyprus (Nicosia: Public Information Office, 1969).

Curry. T and Shibut, L. (eds.). 'The Cost of the Savings and Loan Crisis', *FDIC Banking Review*, XIII (2000), pp. 26–35.

'Cyprus Financial Crisis: the framework for an economic recovery within the eurozone', Speech by Panicos Demetriades, Governor of the Central Bank of Cyprus, at a discussion organised by the Hellenic American Bankers Associ-ation and the Cyprus–US Chamber of Commerce (New York, December 11, 2012).

Data from the 'World Travel and Tourism Economic Impact Report on Cyprus', World Travel and Tourism Council, 2014.

Delia Velculescu speech at The Economist Conference entitled 'Cyprus on the Mend?', November 25, 2013, published online at http://online.wsj.com/news/articles/SB10001424127887324492604579082843940362678.

Draper G. 'The United Nations Force in Cyprus, Military Law and Law', *War Review*, V-VI (1996).

Economic and Financial Affairs Council. 'Single resolution mechanism: Council reviews the state of play of the negotiations', report published February 18, 2014.

Engelen, Klaus C. 'From Deauville to Cyprus', *The Magazine of International Economic Policy* (Spring 2013), pp. 50–53, 73–76.

European Banking Authority 2011 EU-Wide Stress Test Aggregate Report, published on the July 15, 2011, available online http://www.eba.europa.eu/documents/10180/15935/EBA_ST_2011_Summary_Report_v6.pdf/54a9ec8e-3a44-449f-9a5f-e820cc2c2f0, p. 36.

European Central Bank. 'Annual Report' (March 7, 2000), available online at http://www.ecb.europa.eu/pub/pdf/annrep/ar1999en.pdf.

European Central Bank. 'Results of the 2011 EBA EU-wide stress test: Sum-mary, Marfin Popular Bank Co Ltd', available online at http://www.eba.europa.eu/documents/10180/15935/CY006.pdf/e2f3605e-359a-4519-b15b-296ba0d0d2fd.

European Central Bank. 'Results of the 2011 EBA EU-wide stress test: Summary, Piraeus Bank', available online at http://www.eba.europa.eu/documents/10180/15935/GR033.pdf/b8f02648-4beb-4efa-8d61-f02acbc5b666.

European Commission. 'Report on Greek Government Deficit and Debt Statistics', January 2010, p. 4, pp. 27–28.

European Commission of Human Rights, 'Report of the Commission', (Coun-cil of Europe, Application Numbers 678074 and 695075. Cyprus against Turkey. Adopted 10 July 1976).

European Commission report 'Proposal for a Single Resolution Mechanism for the Banking Union', published on the July 10, 2013, available online at http://europa.eu/rapid/press-release_MEMO-13-675_en.htm.

European Banking Authority. 'The European Banking Authority 2011 EU-Wide Stress Test Aggregate Report', published on the July 15, 2011,

see    http://www.eba.europa.eu/documents/10180/15935/EBA_ST_2011_
Summary_Report_v6.pdf/54a9ec8e-3a44-449f-9a5f-e820cc2c2f0a, p. 36.

Fouscas, Vassilis. 'Reflections on the Cyprus Issue and the Turkish Invasions of 1974', *Mediterranean Quarterly*, XII (2001), pp. 98–127.

Higgins, R. 'Basic Facts on the United Nations Force in Cyprus', *The World Today*, 1964.

International Monetary Fund, 'Greece: Ex Post Evaluation of Exceptional Access under the 2010 Stand-By Arrangement', report published in Washington DC, June 2013, available online at http://www.imf.org/external/pubs/ft/scr/2013/cr13156.pdf.

International Monetary Fund, 'IMF Statement on Cyprus', published March 24, 2013, available online at https://www.imf.org/external/np/sec/pr/2013/pr1391.htm.

James, Alan. 'Recent Development in United Nations Peace Keeping', *Yearbook of World Affairs*, XXXI (1977).

Keen, Steve. 'Finance and economic breakdown: modelling Minsky's Financial Instability Hypothesis', *Journal of Post Keynesian Economics*, XVII, pp. 607–635.

Leventis, Yiorghos. 'The Politics of the Cypriot Left in the Inter-War Period: 1918–1940', *Synthesis – Review of Modern Greek Studies*, II (1997), p. 13.

Orphanides, Athanasios. 'What Happened in Cyprus? The Economic Consequences of the Last Communist Government in Europe', MIT Sloan School of Management research paper (May 2014), pp. 7–8.

Pashardes, Panos and Pashaourtidou, Nicoletta. 'Output Loss from the Banking Crisis in Cyprus', *Cyprus Economic Policy Review* (VII), pp. 3–24.

Petmesidou, Maria. 'Cyprus: Annual National Report 2010, Pensions, Health and Long-Term Care', *The European Commission* (May, 2010), p. 10, http://socialprotection.eu/files_db/886/asisp_ANR10_Cyprus.pdf.

Petmesidou, Maria. 'Cyprus: Annual National Report 2011, Pensions, Health and Long-Term Care', *The European Commission* (May, 2011), available online at http://socialprotection.eu/files_db/1100/asisp_ANR11_Cyprus.pdf.

Petmesidou, Maria. 'Cyprus: Annual National Report 2010, Pensions, Health and Long-Term Care', *The European Commission* (2010), available online at http://socialprotection.eu/files_db/886/asisp_ANR10_Cyprus.pdf.

PIMCO. 'Independent Due Diligence of the Banking System of Cyprus', (February 2013), available online at http://www.centralbank.gov.cy/media/pdf/CyprusIndependentDueDiligenceReport_18April.pdf.

Rehn, Ollie. 'Statement on Cyprus in the European Parliament', Strasbourg, April 17, 2013, published online at http://europa.eu/rapid/press-release_SPEECH-13-325_en.htm.

Savvides, Philippos K . 'Cyprus at the Gate of the European Union', ELIAMEP Policy Paper no 1, Athens, June 2002.

Stark , Jurgen. Speech at the Institute of Risk and Regulation, Hong Kong, April 12, 2011.

Theodorides (Theodore), John. 'The Legal Aspects of United Nations Peace Keeping in Cyprus', *War Law Review* (1977).

Theodorides (Theodore), John. 'The United Nations Peacekeeping Force in Cyprus', *The International and Comparative Law Quarterly*, XXXI (1982).

Theodore, John. 'Guidelines for Peacekeeping', *British Army Review*, LXV (1980).

Tocci, Nathalie. 'Reflections on Post-referendum Cyprus', *The International Spectator: Italian Journal of International Affairs* (2008), published online at http://www.tandfonline.com/doi/pdf/10.1080/03932720408457082.

Troika, 'Memorandum of Understanding on Specific Economic Policy Conditionality', published April 12, 2013, available online at http://static.cyprus.com/troika_memo_final.pdf.

United Nations, *Yearbook of the United Nations*, Volumes 27–29 (New York: United Nations Public Information Office, 1973–75).

Wood, Duncan, and Campbell, Alexander. 'Greek Woes Focus Attention on Role of Eurostat', (*Risk* magazine: 2010).

United Nations Security Council Documents – Reports of the Secretary General:

UNFICYP: Document S/5575 186 (1964)
Document S/5950 – September 10, 1964
Document S/6228 – March 11, 1965
Document S/5634 – March 31, 1964
Document S/6102 – December 12, 1964
Document S/9521 – December 3, 1969
Document S/11468 – August 26 – 8th September 8, 1974
Document S/12093 – December 9 1975 – June 5, 1976
Document S/12323 – April 30, 1977
Document S/12463 – April 30, 1977
Document S/12946 – December 1, 1978

# Index

Lightning Source UK Ltd.
Milton Keynes UK
UKOW06n1837160715

255341UK00002B/5/P